Jerrold Northrop Moore

VAUGHAN WILLIAMS

A Life in Photographs

OXFORD   NEW YORK

OXFORD UNIVERSITY PRESS

1992

Oxford University Press, Walton Street, Oxford OX2 6DP

Oxford New York Toronto
Delhi Bombay Calcutta Madras Karachi
Petaling Java Singapore Hong Kong Tokyo
Nairobi Dar es Salaam Cape Town
Melbourne Auckland
and associated companies in
Berlin Ibadan

Oxford is a trade mark of Oxford University Press

Published in the United States
by Oxford University Press, New York

British Library Cataloguing in Publication Data
Data available

Library of Congress Cataloging in Publication Data
Vaughan Williams, a life in photographs / Jerrold Northrop Moore.
1. Vaughan Williams, Ralph, 1872–1958—Pictorial works.
2. Composers—England—Pictorial works.   I. Title.
ML88.V39M66   1992   780'.92—dc20   92–15513
ISBN 0–19–816296–0

Printed in Hong Kong

Preface

THE Pictorial Biography which John Lunn and I compiled in 1971 was in the nature of a family album—faces from home, school, university, war, many musical occasions, and friends from each part of a long and creative life.

Jerrold Northrop Moore has taken a different view, and has related the composer's life to his times. It is seen against the patterns of a changing world in which the music started, developed, and grew, exploring and discovering through every phase of RVW's work.

The imaginative backgrounds belong not only to the composer's time, but to the influences which touched his imagination; so they give a different and wider perspective to his experience.

Only the final pages in these books are similar. In both, RVW's translation from Horace ends the text. The coda from his *Songs of Travel*, a poem by Stevenson, also sums up the completed years recorded in this book:

> I have trod the upward and the downward path,
>   I have endured and done in days before.
> I have longed for all and bid farewell to hope—
>   And I have lived and loved and closed the door.

Ursula Vaughan Williams.

Erasmus Darwin (1731–1802) was a physician and poet of 'The Botanic Garden'.

The view below is taken from his 'Plan for the Conduct of Female Education in Boarding Schools' (1797). Amongst its recommendations for objects of arts and science to be shown to the young ladies was the Wedgwood Pottery (opposite).

Darwin's great-great-grandson was Ralph Vaughan Williams. When Vaughan Williams's wife saw this portrait by Joseph Wright of Derby, she wrote:

Dr Darwin's hands might have been painted from Ralph's own.

Josiah Wedgwood (1730–95), another great-great-grandfather, founded the world's most celebrated pottery at Stoke-on-Trent.

For the factory, Wedgwood's friend Erasmus Darwin designed a celebrated windmill.

Wedgwood himself was equally versatile. His portrait by Sir Joshua Reynolds shows a remarkable anticipation of his great-great-grandson's features.

The Wedgwood and Darwin families were to be linked several times by marriage. The wedding of Josiah Wedgwood III and Caroline Darwin in 1837 produced three daughters. One was to become the mother of Ralph Vaughan Williams.

Leith Hill Place

In 1847 Josiah Wedgwood (grandson of the potter) bought Leith Hill Place, built about 1730 on the edge of the Surrey Downs.

It made a comfortable home for his wife Caroline (a sister of Charles Darwin) and their daughters Sophy, Margaret, and Lucy.

The nurseries were in the attics of the house—a kingdom from which the little girls descended sedately to say good morning to their parents, and to receive a teaspoon of cream from the grown-ups' breakfast table.

They grew up in an easy world, with the discipline, good manners, and sense of responsibility towards those less fortunate than themselves usual in such households.

Margaret at thirteen, 1856.

Tanhurst

The hall at Tanhurst, with Lady Vaughan Williams, and one of her six sons running up the stairs.

Built on the slopes of Leith Hill, Tanhurst was the nearest house to Leith Hill Place. It had been taken by Sir Edward Vaughan Williams for his young family of six sons and a daughter. Asked the reason for his choice of this district, Sir Edward answered:

Because it is full of charming young heiresses.

Arthur Vaughan Williams, the third son, was born in 1834. He followed his elder brothers to Westminster School. In 1854 he went up to Christ Church, Oxford. There his great friend was Herbert Fisher (whose daughter was years later to marry Arthur's son).

Arthur took his BA in 1857 and MA three years later. After early posts at Bemerton (George Herbert's parish near Salisbury) and Halsall, Lancashire, in 1865 he was made vicar of Alverstoke in Hampshire. From there it was easier to get home to Tanhurst and to visit Leith Hill Place.

Both families were pleased when Arthur and Margaret Wedgwood became engaged in September 1867.

At the New Year 1868 Arthur Vaughan Williams accepted the living at Down Ampney, Gloucestershire. He and Margaret were married on 22 February, and they moved into the vicarage.

For the birth of their first child Hervey, in the summer of 1869, Margaret returned to Leith Hill Place.

BAPTISMS solemnized in the Parish of *Down Ampney* in the County of *Gloucester* in the year One thousand eight hundred and

When Baptized.	Child's Christian Name.	Parents' Name.		Abode.	Quality, Trade, or Profession.	By whom the Ceremony was performed
		Christian	Surname			
18 72 Sept 22d	Emma Matilda	William & Sarah	Turner	Down Ampney	Sawyer	R. Vaughan Williams (Vicar)
No. 73						
18 72 October 13	Ernest Henry	Henry & Matilda	Richens	Down Ampney	Groom	R. Vaughan Williams (Vicar)
No. 74						
18 72 December 1st	Ralph	Arthur & Margaret	Vaughan Williams	Down Ampney	Vicar	Hyde H. Beadon Offg. Minr.
No. 75						
18 72 December 2		Reuben & Hannah		Down Ampney	Labourer	R. Vaughan Williams (Vicar)
No. 76						
18 73						R. Vaughan Williams (Vicar)
						R. Vaughan Williams (Vicar)

The two younger children were born at the Vicarage, Down Ampney. After Meggie (1871) Ralph was born on 12 October 1872. He was baptised three weeks later.

Ralph

Arthur Vaughan Williams was much liked at Down Ampney. Beside
his parish work, he taught Arithmetic as well as Scripture and
Catechism at the village school.

Early in February 1875 he fell ill without warning. After an illness of
only two days, on the afternoon of 9 February Arthur Vaughan
Williams died.

   Ralph was hardly more than two. He was to keep only a dim
memory of his father. But this loss led to another: departure from the
house of his birth and the scenes of all his own experience thus far.

After Arthur's death, Margaret took their children back to live with her parents at Leith Hill Place. They had a visit from Margaret's aunt by marriage, the wife of Charles Darwin. Aunt Emma wrote:

I sat out with them most of the time, and Margaret soon joined us. She looks very thin and speaks in a low voice as if she was weak, but was quite calm and joined in everything; she looks very pretty in her widow's cap. Hervey was playing about all the time and the other two came after. Little Ralph has regular features . . .

Leith Hill Place servants. Their individualities were cherished by the family most of them served throughout their working lives.

Front row (*left to right*): Mark Cook (gardener), Sarah Wager (nurse), Annie Longhurst, Joseph Berry. Philips the butler stands in the centre at the back.

The children had settled into the old nursery in the attic, and their nurse, Sarah Wager, was Ralph's friend in particular . . . She was a passionate radical and planted her political ideas in the nursery. They were not unlike those of her employers . . .

Hervey and Meggie;
Ralph (1876)

11

Ralph was given his first music lessons at Leith Hill Place. There his mother's sister Sophy took him through 'A Child's Introduction to Thorough Bass' (1819).

When he was six he began his career as a composer with a four-bar piano piece. He called it 'The Robin's Nest'.

After a visit from the Vaughan Williams children, Charles Darwin wrote to their mother

. . . to tell you of a trait of Ralph more than amusing—when I gave his tip I said, 'Don't mention it till you are in the carriage.'

He presently afterwards said to me, 'I suppose I ought to give it back to you for I have told Aunt Sophy.'

A proof of pleasure which he could not forbear to show, and of honesty which he could not resist.

Ralph asked his mother about 'The Origin of Species', and what it meant. She answered:

'The Bible says that God made the world in six days, Great Uncle Charles thinks it took longer: but we need not worry about it, for it is equally wonderful either way.'

This answer completely satisfied Ralph at this time: nor did he ever forget it, for it seemed typical of her good sense, bringing difficult problems within the scope of the children's understanding.

Among the books of Ralph's childhood was a family Shakespeare: it was to stay with him all his life.

The illustrations included music mentioned in the plays. In 'The Merry Wives of Windsor' was the old tune of 'Greensleeves'.

² SCENE I. (also ACT V. Sc. V.)—" *Green sleeves.*"

This appears to have been a very popular song in Shakspere's time, and, judging from an allusion to it in Fletcher's Tragi-Comedy, 'The Loyal Subject,' as well as from a pamphlet entered at Stationers' Hall, in February, 1580, under the title of 'A representation against *Green Sleeves*, by W. Elderton,' was thought gross, even in an age when what was in gay society called polite conversation was rarely free from

Ralph's interest in plays found focus in a toy theatre. For its dramas he wrote a whole book of 'Overtures by Mr. R. V. Williams', dated 5 June 1882. One was 'The Galoshes of Happienes'.

When Ralph was seven, he began violin lessons with an old German music teacher called Cramer . . . He soon discovered that he felt much happier with a stringed instrument than he had ever done with the pianoforte.

Then he decided to orchestrate 'The Galoshes of Happienes'.

14

Another revelation came after a winter party. It was rather late in the evening and the children were bundled into the carriage, wrapped in rugs for the drive home. The others slept, but Ralph, fascinated by the moonlit frosty night and the sound of the hoofs on the road, stayed awake.

He heard the sound of a bell as they drove by a village church. The regular tolling at this strange hour filled him with wonder, and he asked why it should ring at night and so slowly.

Sarah explained it was the passing bell, and told him it was ringing for someone who had just died.

And thus it could toll him back to the passing at Down Ampney now hardly remembered, and the loss of all his earliest life.

A high brick wall enclosed four acres of land as a kitchen garden with glass houses and potting sheds next to the home farm. Here, and in orchards and coach houses there was endless scope for games and adventure.

The Leith Hill Place gardener, Mark Cook

15

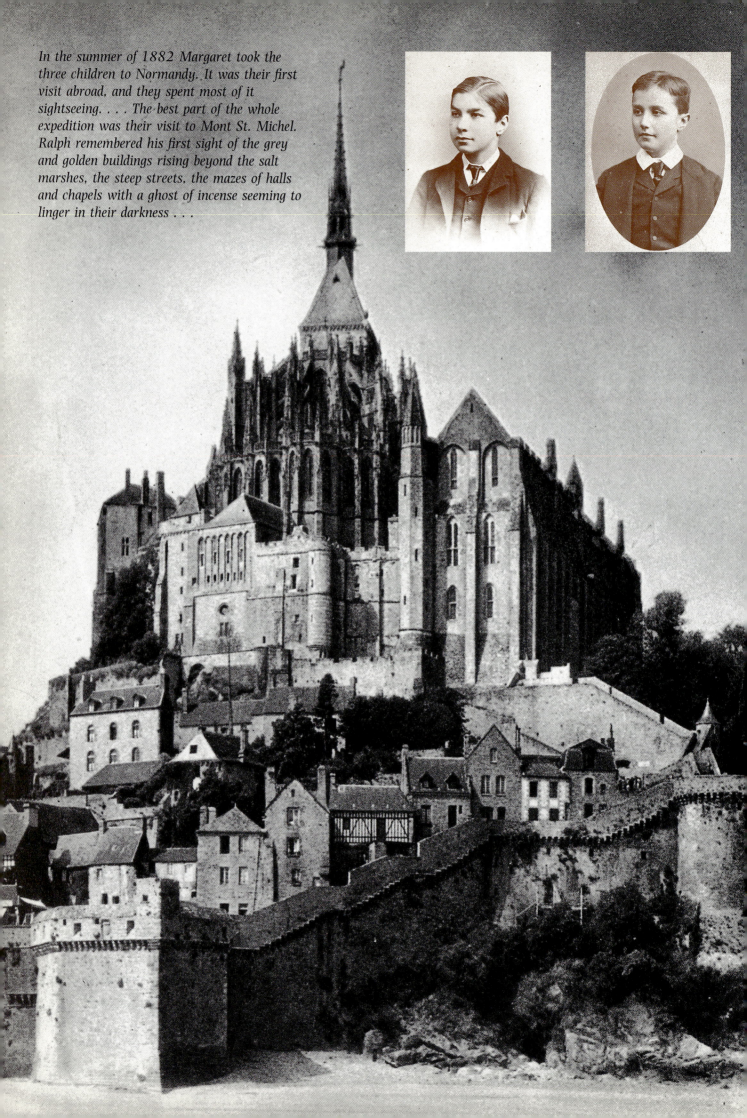

In the summer of 1882 Margaret took the three children to Normandy. It was their first visit abroad, and they spent most of it sightseeing. . . . The best part of the whole expedition was their visit to Mont St. Michel. Ralph remembered his first sight of the grey and golden buildings rising beyond the salt marshes, the steep streets, the mazes of halls and chapels with a ghost of incense seeming to linger in their darkness . . .

Besides having his music lessons with his Aunt Sophy, Ralph played duets with his brother and sister from
'. . . funny old volumes containing choruses from "Messiah" and "Israel in Egypt", and arias from "Don Giovanni" and the overture to "Figaro", which we used to play Andante Sostenuto!'
When Ralph and Meggie first heard works from their repertoire played by orchestras, the pace seemed slightly shocking.

Now Hervey had gone away to school, only Meggie was left for daily company— together with their mother, their aunt, and the servants. Ralph found his fulfilment in music and the companionship of books.

Hervey (*left*), Ralph, and Meggie (*right*)

There were other holiday journeys, sometimes to the Three Choirs Festivals where Ralph heard choral music for the first time.

He had become passionately interested in architecture, and he explored books about Norman and Gothic buildings, lecturing Meggie and Sarah Wager on any castles or cathedrals they visited.

His mother gave him a well-illustrated and informative 'Pictorial History of the British Isles' for Christmas in 1883.

PICTORIAL ARCHITECTURE OF THE BRITISH ISLES.

accepted Gothic plan. The Gothic builders almost universally adopted a scheme of plan and section which, though of unequalled beauty, was inconsistent with the fundamental principle of Gothic design. That principle I take to be this — that no pressure must be left unbalanced. The thrust of the main vault was resisted on each side by flying buttresses. In England these are often within the triforium, beneath the protecting roofs of as they are at Westminster, and the upper range too high—often indeed not only absolutely useless, but even mischievous— being above the point where the support is needed, and confusing the lines of the upper portion of the building. However, the object is usually attained, and the lateral thrust of the main vault effectually met.

In the aisles the vault pressure is resisted on the one side by the external buttresses,

GLOUCESTER CATHEDRAL.

the aisles;—as in the nave of Wells. Where this is the case the expression of the exterior is that of perfect repose ; and the building is secured against the peril in which the insidious action of the weather upon these buttresses must necessarily involve it. In other instances, we have a single range of buttresses above the aisle roofs, and thus forming a noticeable feature in the external view ; as at Exeter. Abroad they are generally double, But what becomes of it on the other ? It appears to have been altogether disregarded, as of no account. Yet you may enter church after church, and, looking upwards along the vaulting shafts, find that they are not straight but bowed — pushed inwards towards the nave at the triforium level by the pressure of the aisle vaulting, and outwards at the clearstory by that of the main avenue :—or perhaps generally rather that the pressure of the

This interest bore fruit in later years when he studied the work of Tudor composers, for he found then that he was familiar with another aspect of their world . . .

Field House School, Rottingdean: 1883–1886

In September 1883, when he was nearly eleven, he followed Hervey to Field House School. It gave Ralph his first sustained contact with boys of his own age.

The boys had a fairly hard life. They got up at half past six for half an hour of preparation, followed by practice of a musical instrument (which excused the player from prayers) before eight o'clock breakfast which consisted of tea, bread and butter with a small piece of cold beef.

There were lessons all the morning, then luncheon—large and coarse joints and lots of stodge-pudding. The boys went to a shop near by for kippers and chocolate with pink cream inside to supplement Miss Hewitt's housekeeping economies.

Games and walks filled the afternoon, followed by tea and bread and butter at five, and after that preparation, punctuated by baths once a week.

Even at school, Ralph's constant companion was music:

The music teaching, by two visiting masters from Brighton, was very good. I learned pianoforte from Mr A. C. West who, after giving me one or two ordinary pieces, realised I was more musical than most of his boys, and introduced me to a delightful little volume called 'The Bach Album' . . .

My violin master was [an Irishman] called Quirke, a fine player and a good teacher, but not a very cultivated musician. He made me learn Raff's 'Cavatina', which was the fashionable piece at that moment, and I played it at a school concert.

The year after I again appeared at a school concert and played the rather too popular Bach-Gounod 'Prelude'.

He found companionship also in the surrounding landscape:

Most of the boys thought the country round was dull. I thought it lovely and enjoyed our walks. The great bare hills impressed me by their grandeur. I have loved the Downs ever since.

Field House, 1886: Ralph is seventh from the left, in the second row from the back.

PART I.

PROLOGUE	... ...	W. Wakeford, Esq.
	A. W. CHURCHILL.	
CHORUS	"The Old Brigade."	O. Barri.
VIOLIN TRIO ...	... ...	...
	R. V. WILLIAMS, H. PHILLIPS, H. G. LEWIN.	
TRIO ...	... Cradle Song ...	Taubert.
VIOLIN SOLO ...	... ...	Gounod.
	R. V. WILLIAMS.	
PART SONG	... "The Legend of the Bells." ...	From Les Cloches de Corneville.
BALLAD (with chorus)	"The Primrose." ...	F. Abt.
	A. W. EDGELOW, H. O. CLARKE, R. T. GODMAN.	
TRIO ...	... "Evening." ...	H. Smart.
CANTATA	... "ROBIN HOOD." ...	Leroy.
RECITATION ...	From "The Heir at Law." ...	Colman.
	W. T. SUTTHERY, Esq.	
VIOLIN SOLO ...	... ... Scotch Airs. ...	Sainton.
	W. M. QUIRKE, Esq.	
Accompanist	- - - - - W. W. HEWITT, Esq.	

MUSICAL SKETCH:

A RURAL HOLIDAY,

C. T. WEST, Esq.

'Musical and Dramatic Entertainment', Field House, 15 December 1886.

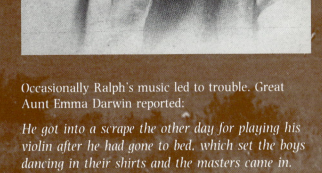

Occasionally Ralph's music led to trouble. Great Aunt Emma Darwin reported:

He got into a scrape the other day for playing his violin after he had gone to bed, which set the boys dancing in their shirts and the masters came in.

Charterhouse: 1887–1890

There were in my time two presiding authorities over Carthusian music: Mr G. H. Robinson, the organist, and Mr Becker who taught the pianoforte and also played the horn. Robinson was a sensitive musician and a kind-hearted man, and gave me leave to practise on the chapel organ.

In weekly practices of the school orchestra . . . one of my first practical lessons in orchestration came from playing the viola part in Beethoven's First Symphony, when I was excited to find that my repeated notes on the viola were enriched by a long holding note from Mr Becker's horn.

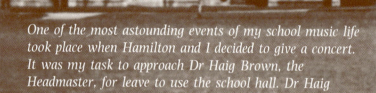

One of the most astounding events of my school music life took place when Hamilton and I decided to give a concert. It was my task to approach Dr Haig Brown, the Headmaster, for leave to use the school hall. Dr Haig

G. H. Robinson with the boys of his house, 1889. To the left of the master sits the monitor of the Robinites, Ralph.

20

Then there was, of course, the school choir which practised once a week in the time otherwise devoted to extra French, and was therefore very popular. Choir and orchestra used to meet once a year for a grand concert at the end of the summer, and occasionally for an oratorio. I remember taking part in 'Judas Maccabaeus'.

Brown was a formidable man, and in later life I should never have dared to make the request, but leave was obtained . . .

Partly as a result of this concert, Girdlestone (who organized the Sunday evening 'Entertas') decided to devote four of them to national programmes and I was ordered to provide a Welsh concert. This was my first introduction to the beautiful melodies of the Principality.

CHARTERHOUSE,

Sunday, August 5th, 1888.

Programme.

Pianoforte Duet	{ Rondo from Quartet in C minor } ...	Spohr.

H. W. C. Erskine and J. G. S. Mellor.

Song ... ... "The Chorister" ... ... Sullivan.
B. G. Branston.

Trio ... ... in G ... R. V. Williams.
H. V. Hamilton { B. K. R. Wilkinson / R. V. Williams } S. Massingberd.

Song ... "There is a green hill far away" Gounod.
Mr. L. Marshall.

Pianoforte Solo } ... Phantaisie in A ... ... Bach.
Mr. Robinson.

Song ... "I dreamt I was in Heaven" H. V. Hamilton.
B. G. Branston.

Quartet ... ... No. 5 .. .. Haydn.
J. E. Bidwell, A. G. G. Cowie, T. Shaw, C. M. Rayner.

Air ... ... From the "Creation" ... Haydn.
Mr. Bode.

Duet for two Pianofortes } Sonata in D ... ... Mozart.
H. V. Hamilton and N. G. Smith.

Royal College of Music: 1890–1892

Ralph felt he had the makings of a good string player. He had given up the violin for the viola, an instrument he loved; and he would have dearly liked to become an orchestral player.

But the whole weight of family opinion was against him. If he had to be a musician, he must be an organist—which was a safe and respectable career.

So with dogged determination he worked at the organ . . .

In the spring of 1890 Ralph persuaded his mother to let him leave Charterhouse and go to the Royal College of Music in London.

Mrs Vaughan Williams agreed reluctantly. But she insisted that her younger son live at home in Leith Hill Place.

So at the age of eighteen Ralph became a commuter.

I was determined if possible to study composition under Parry . . .
I got to know some of his music, especially 'Judith', and I
remember saying to my mother that there was something, to my
mind, peculiarly English in his music.

After two terms I passed my Grade V harmony and was
allowed to become a pupil of Parry. I will not try to describe what
this experience meant to a boy . . .

One day he was talking to me about the wonderful climax of the
'Appassionata' Sonata. Suddenly he realized that I did not know it,
so he sat down at the pianoforte and played it through to me.
There were showers of wrong notes, but in spite of that it was the
finest performance that I have ever heard.

Parry was very generous in lending scores to his pupils. (This
was long before the day of miniature scores and gramophone
records). I borrowed 'Siegfried' and 'Tristan' and Brahms's
'Requiem', and for some time after my compositions consisted
entirely of variations of a passage near the beginning of that work.

At Covent Garden in June 1892, Mahler
conducted the first English performance
of *Tristan und Isolde* in many years.
Ralph went to it and was
deeply shaken.

Trinity College, Cambridge: 1892–1895

Cambridge gave Ralph the right life precisely when he was ready to appreciate it. He was fortunate in his contemporaries, particularly in his cousin Ralph Wedgwood, who came from Clifton to Trinity fully fledged with worldly knowledge and with friendships already established. The two Ralphs shared Darwin relations at Cambridge to whose houses they were both welcome. . . .

Ralph's official study was history, a subject chosen because the lectures at Cambridge did not conflict with Parry's teaching days at the R.C.M.: he spent as much time on music as he could . . .

The independence of living away from home was intoxicating. Besides music and history, conversation and cousins, there were girls. All through his life Ralph was romantically susceptible to beauty, and at Cambridge he was as liable to fall in love as any one of his age. . . .

Another house at which he was always welcome was the Lodge at Downing. The Vaughan Williams and Fisher families had been friends since Ralph's father and uncles had known Herbert Fisher at Christ Church . . . The eldest of Herbert Fisher's daughters, Florence, had married Frederic Maitland, who held the Chair of the Laws of England, and there was a great deal of music-making in their home at Downing College. . . .

Sometimes Florence's younger sister Adeline stayed at the Lodge. She was able to play the cello if no one else was available to do so, though her real talent was for the piano . . .

Undergraduate reading party at a holiday house taken by
G. M. Trevelyan for friends. *Left to right*: Ralph Wedgwood,
Maurice Amos, G. E. Moore, Trevelyan, and RVW
(drawn by Amos, anticipating a dreamt-of reunion in 1930).

The dedication of the holiday Log Book was headed by a pun
connecting their host's initials with Greenwich Mean Time.

'G.M.T.' (coupled with) 'Posterity'

To these two names these pages are dedicated by the writers:
The one, that of him who granted the first charter of our
  liberties, and made over the territory upon whose border,
  Reader, you stand.
By Posterity, whom can we mean, if not our After-Selves?
  Can we hope that they may have a certain charity for
  the Authors?

Posterity was to distribute among the five undergraduates two
Knighthoods and three Orders of Merit.

Cousins at Cambridge:
Ralph ('Randolph') Wedgwood and RVW.

Ralph had taken his B.Mus in 1894, so he left Cambridge with a solid achievement and returned to the Royal College of Music . . .

Parry was now Director of the R.C.M., so Ralph went to Stanford for lessons.

Stanford was a great teacher, but I believe I was unteachable. . . . The details of my work annoyed Stanford so much that we seldom got beyond these to the broader issues, and the lesson usually started with a conversation on these lines:

'Damnably ugly, my boy. Why do you write such things?'

'Because I like them.'

'But you can't like them, they're not music.'

'I shouldn't write them if I didn't like them.'

Stanford tried—I fear in vain—to lighten my texture. He actually made me write a waltz. I was much bitten by the modes at that time, and I produced a modal waltz!

. . . I once showed him a movement of a quartet which had caused me hours of agony, and I really thought it was going to move mountains this time.

'All rot, my boy,' was his only comment.

What one really learns from an Academy or College is not so much from one's official teachers as from one's fellow students. I was lucky in my companions in those days. Other students at the College were Dunhill, Ireland, Howard-Jones, Fritz Hart, and Gustav von Holst.

We used to meet at a little teashop in Kensington and discuss every subject under the sun from the lowest note of the double bassoon to the philosophy of 'Jude the Obscure'. I learnt more from those conversations than from any amount of formal teaching.

Chief among these friendships was that with Gustav von Holst. He was two years younger than Ralph, and he came from a family of professional musicians. From the first they seemed to be complementary in character, and Ralph spoke of him as 'the greatest influence on my music'. . . .

From their College days they started playing their works over to each other for criticism and help—'field days' which became more important to both as time went on.

Yet Holst shared some basic characteristics with Ralph. The most important was his own romantic outlook. That was to emerge in the use Holst made of modal writing and folk song—as well as in the younger man's unfulfilling marriage.

He was fortunate because an allowance from his family saved him from the necessity of having to earn his living.

    . . . In spite of this he took an organist's post in 1895 at the church of St. Barnabas, South Lambeth . . . He had rooms in St. Barnabas Villas [below].

. . . I never could play the organ. But this post gave me an insight into good and bad church music, which stood me in good stead later on.

    I also founded a choral society and an orchestral society, both of them pretty bad, but we managed once to do a Bach Cantata, and I obtained some of the practical knowledge of music which is so essential to a composer's make-up.

At this time Ralph was rather a dandy, with a liking for the fashionable, large, floppy ties. He was tall, broad-shouldered, and good-looking, with dark hair that curled a little unless he kept it cut very short, and eyes, between grey and blue, that looked bluer in summer when he was sunburned.

After three years in 'this damned place' he would try to persuade his friend von Holst to take it on:

I consider it more important to take every chance of improving one's talents (?!?) than to save one's soul.

Under the bluff exterior Ralph was discovering atheism. Perhaps it was part of the man's response to the child's loss of a father in the church.

He found a deepening interest in Adeline Fisher. Adeline was one of eleven children.
Her mother (whose sister was the mother of Virginia Stephen, later Virginia Woolf)
came from a family of

. . . immense clannishness, a cult of family so passionate and intense that
even the husbands and wives they married remained outsiders . . .
    'Adeline could have married anyone,' was often said,
but quite obviously she didn't want to, and no one
succeeded in touching what many must have
believed a heart of ice.

A magnet for both Fishers and Stephens
was Virginia's half-sister, Stella Duckworth.
Stella became a second mother to the Stephen girls,
and she was probably Adeline's closest confidante.
    One of Stella's brothers had made advances to Virginia when
she was only a child, causing permanent psychic damage. In April 1897
Stella married: her young husband was over-ardent, and she returned from the
honeymoon severely ill.
    Adeline immediately went to stay at the Stephens' home to nurse Stella.

Shyness and the conventions of romance—the inaccessibility of distant beauty, almost in the mediaeval troubadour manner—were Ralph's natural element.

This was a curious paradox in a man of passionate disposition and warm human affection, who all his life enjoyed both the decorative gaieties and the lively companionship of women . . .

Brought up in the rigid moral code of his age, he admired the freer ways of others . . . But any physical indulgence was impossible or inhibited for him by his own inner discipline, which . . . forbade anything that he thought might hurt or injure another person.

Thus it was that Adeline's detached manner could appeal to a young man of Ralph's inexperience as giving their affair some special formality. Formality offers a measure of safety: and so her remoteness might acquire the power of actually fostering their relationship in his romantic mind.

Croquet and music
with Cambridge friends

Ivor Gatty (horn), René Gatty
(violin), Ralph (viola), Adeline
(cello), Nicholas Gatty (violin)

Adeline was nursing Stella when Ralph proposed and was accepted. The young couple shared many interests and their families were old friends, though the Fishers did not enjoy the prospect of another break in their close family circle.

Then Stella's illness worsened, and she died on 19 July 1897, only three months after marriage.

Adeline's grief and despair excluded everything else, and nearly brought her own engagement to an end. No one can know what confidences had been exchanged between the young women, but Stella's resentment almost certainly played a part in Adeline's unhappiness.

. . . After the funeral she went to stay with Ralph's grandmother, Lady Vaughan Williams, at Queen Anne's Gate, and while there she managed to come to terms with life, though the happiness of the first bright days was never wholly recaptured.

On 9 October 1897 Ralph and Adeline were married at the Parish Church, All Saints, Hove . . . Ralph Wedgwood was the best man. Adeline was twenty-seven, and Ralph would be twenty-five three days later.

Adeline's parents and some of her family went to San Remo early in December. Adeline and Ralph joined them there for Christmas.

On the way, changing trains at Bolzano, they had time for a long walk, and Adeline took a romantic photograph of Ralph lying on the sunny hillside.

The year 1902 brought the Boer War to an end. Adeline's brother Jack returned home suffering from what was later known as shell shock: he had been full of life and gaiety, but he came back wrecked and destroyed . . .

The months before his death were so agonizing to the family . . . As usual, much of the burden fell on Adeline. Her passionate devotion helped them all through the first break in the enchanted family circle—though it told on her, and indirectly on Ralph, who could help her only by leaving her entirely free to be where she felt she belonged.

He sought a different focus for his art in the Pre-Raphaelite poetry of the Rossettis. During 1902 and 1903 he set fifteen of their poems. One of these settings of longing, 'Silent Noon', reached out for a whole moment of satisfied love.

SILENT NOON.

Your hands lie open in the long fresh grass,—
　The finger-points look through like rosy blooms :
　Your eyes smile peace.　The pasture gleams and glooms
'Neath billowing skies that scatter and amass.
All round our nest, far as the eye can pass,
　Are golden kingcup-fields with silver edge
　Where the cow-parsley skirts the hawthorn-hedge.
'Tis visible silence, still as the hour-glass.

Deep in the sun-searched growths the dragon-fly
Hangs like a blue thread loosened from the sky :—
　So this wing'd hour is dropt to us from above.
Oh ! clasp we to our hearts, for deathless dower,
This close-companioned inarticulate hour
　When twofold silence was the song of love.

He turned to poetry of triumphant loneliness in Whitman's 'Leaves of Grass':

Down from the gardens of Asia descending,
Adam and Eve appear, then their myriad
　progeny after them,
Wandering, yearning, with restless explorations,
　questionings, baffled, formless, feverish, with
　never-happy hearts that sad incessant refrain,—
'Wherefore unsatisfied soul?
Whither O mocking life?'

But for such a question he could find no setting then—and so, no answer.

A partial answer seemed to come from the country around Leith Hill Place. Nearby neighbours there, the Broadwoods of Lyne, had for years collected traditional folk songs. They wrote them down from the singing of just such old people as the servants Ralph had known from his childhood.

Folk song offered a musical innocence that could touch his deepest feelings about himself. The heritage of English folk song struck Ralph as a subject of such promise that he began to lecture about it:

Great composers in all times in the history of music have not disdained to use folk songs as a means of inspiration . . .

It is extraordinarily interesting to see the national temperament running through every form of a nation's art—the national life and the national art growing together.

The old gardener Mark Cook with his granddaughter on the camomile lawn at Leith Hill Place

Folk song was at the back of Ralph's mind even when he determined to write a pot-boiler.

One day at Leith Hill Place he went for a walk through a field, sat down on a large stone, and sketched out in his book a setting of 'Linden Lea' by the Dorset poet William Barnes.

When 'Linden Lea' was accepted for the first number of a new magazine called *The Vocalist*, appearing in April 1902, it became his first published work. He was twenty-nine.

Soon well-known singers as well as amateurs began to take it up.

Ralph gave his lectures on 'The History of Folk Song' as university extension courses at Pokesdown in Dorset, at Gloucester, and in December 1903 at Brentwood in Essex:

After one talk two middle-aged ladies told him that their father, the vicar of Ingrave, was giving a tea-party for the old people of the village, and some of them possibly might know country songs . . .

The vicar's daughters introduced him to an elderly labourer, Mr Pottipher, who said of course he could not sing at this sort of party, but if Ralph would visit him next day he would be delighted to sing to him then.

The next day Mr Pottipher sang 'Bushes and Briars'. When Ralph heard it, he felt it was something he had known all his life.

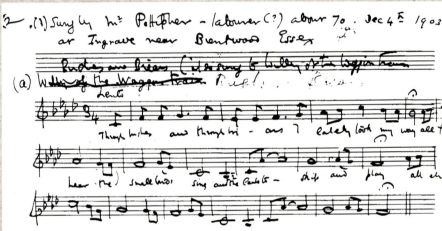

Soon he found himself in the forefront of the movement to collect the folk song heritage of England from the singing of the last generation who preserved them in memory.

Ralph bicycled in East Anglia, finding many of the older country people who would sing songs they had learned from parents and grandparents.

At King's Lynn in January 1905 the Rev F. W. Bussel introduced two fishermen. One of them, Mr Carter, sang 'The Captain's Apprentice'.

It was one of the tunes Ralph loved most, and he used it in a 'Norfolk Rhapsody' for orchestra.

One of Ralph's Folk Music lectures was on church music. A listener described it:

After a very able summary of what folk music had done for religious music, the lecturer touched on modern church music— and made a well-deserved attack on the false sentimentalism of many of our modern hymns, as compared with the true feeling and dignity of earlier examples.

Then a practical opportunity literally walked in at the door:

It must have been in 1904 that I was sitting in my study in Barton Street, Westminster, when a cab drove up to the door and 'Mr Dearmer' was announced. I just knew his name vaguely as a parson who invited tramps to sleep in his drawing room . . .

He went straight to the point and asked me to edit the music of a hymn book. . . .

I thought it over for twenty-four hours and then decided to accept.

I found the work occupied me two years, and that my bill for clerical expenses alone came to about two hundred and fifty pounds.

The truth is that I determined to do the work thoroughly, and that, besides being a compendium of all the tunes of worth that were already in use, the book should, in addition, be a thesaurus of all the finest hymn tunes in the world . . .

When I found a tune for which no English words were available, I took it to Dearmer, as literary editor, and told him that he must write or get somebody else to write suitable words.

When a better tune was needed, Ralph searched the folk melodies collected by himself and colleagues in the Folk Song Society. Failing a discovery there, he turned to old English composers such as Tallis and Gibbons, or to friends like von Holst and John Ireland.

I also, contrary to my principles, contributed a few tunes of my own, but with becoming modesty I attributed them to my old friend, Mr Anon.

One of his own tunes for the Hymnal he named 'Down Ampney'. Another became the most famous of his hymns, 'For all the Saints'.

The English Hymnal was designed for every church that would have it from highest to lowest.

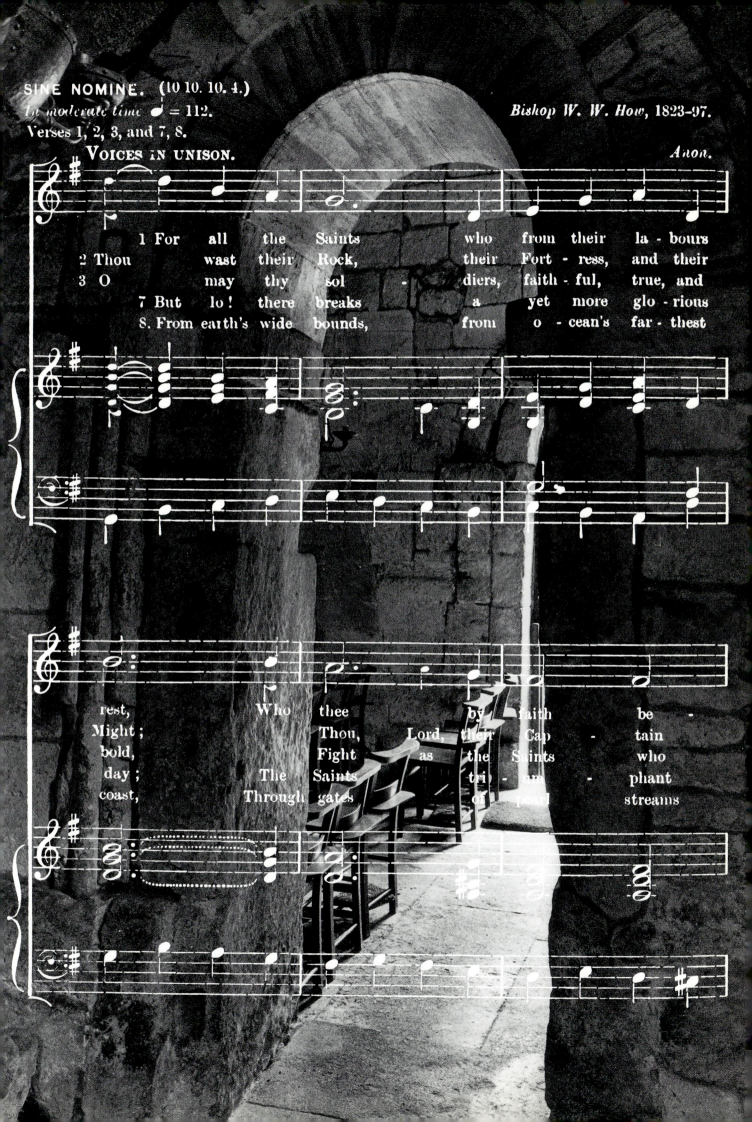

The Leith Hill Festival after more than forty years, with the original seven choirs grown to twenty-four, but Ralph still conducting.

In 1905 Ralph accepted the conductorship of a new competition festival for choirs in the Leith Hill district. A leading role was taken by his sister Meggie, still living with their mother at Leith Hill Place.

Meggie, the Festival Secretary, was indefatigable. She and Ralph bicycled to all the villages, took rehearsals during the winter months, and helped the village conductors in their work.

Another local venture was a performance of scenes from 'Pilgrim's Progress', being acted by friends at Reigate Priory.
   Ralph's music for this was limited by the instruments available . . . and his work had to be within the scope of the singers and players.
   But he found the acting version of the story, not re-read since nursery days, full of dramatic possibility for an opera.

Ruth Charrington as 'Faithful'

Adeline's widowed mother now lived in Chelsea. There Adeline spent part of every day with her. So when the lease at Barton Street came to an end in 1905, they found a house at 13 Cheyne Walk, Chelsea.

The move to Cheyne Walk was the beginning of Ralph's maturity. His study on the top floor of the house with its view across to Battersea Park, of sunsets over the river, and of the river itself, was the room where some of his most important work was to be done.

After a week spent in arranging the house and taking books upstairs to his new study, Ralph went to Leith Hill Place to spend a few days in song collecting.

I could imagine a much less profitable way of spending a long winter evening than in the parlour of a country inn taking one's turn at the mug of 'four-ale', in the rare company of minds imbued with that fine sense which comes from advancing years and a life-long companionship with nature—and with the ever-present chance of picking up some rare old ballad or an exquisitely beautiful melody . . .

All this time he had been working slowly at his project for a big choral and orchestral setting of Whitman. The subject, he decided, should be the ocean. He consulted von Holst:

Gustav and I were both stuck—so I suggested we should both set the same words in competition . . .

The verses chosen for this smaller work convey much of Ralph at this time:

'*No map there, nor guide,*
Nor voice sounding, nor touch of human hand,
Nor face with blooming flesh, nor lips, nor eyes,
 are in that land . . .
All waits undreamed of in that region,
 that inaccessible land.'

Toward the Unknown Region was Ralph's first sizeable choral work. It was accepted for the Leeds Festival, where he conducted the first performance in October 1907. Its success there was a harbinger for the 'Sea Symphony' three years later.

Despite the friendship with von Holst, it was a lonely school:

I learnt almost entirely what I have learnt by trying it on the dog.

Ralph was going to seek lessons with d'Indy in Paris when a friend suggested Maurice Ravel.

Ravel was more than two years Ralph's junior, but was gaining fame with a lengthening list of published works. Ralph wrote to him, spent the winter of 1907–8 in Paris, and went to Ravel four or five times a week:

I learned much from him. For example, that the heavy contrapuntal Teutonic manner was not necessary. 'Complexe mais non compliqué' was his motto.

I practised chiefly orchestration with him. He showed me how to orchestrate in points of colour rather than in lines.

[Ravel was] exactly what I was looking for. As far as I know my own faults, he hit on them exactly, and [told] me to do exactly what I half felt in my mind I ought to do—but it just wanted saying.

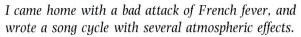

I came home with a bad attack of French fever, and wrote a song cycle with several atmospheric effects.

The songs were from A. E. Housman's 'A Shropshire Lad'. Ralph's settings mixed his new techniques with the accents of traditional English tunes. He called his songs *On Wenlock Edge*.

In September 1908 Ralph went to collect songs in Herefordshire. One of the singers he found was Mrs Caroline Bridges of Pembridge. She was a singer of carols, and two of the Herefordshire carols made a basis for Ralph's *Fantasia on Christmas Carols* four years later.

Adeline had not been well for a long time. She suffered from rheumatic or arthritic pain, and she was no longer able to go for bicycle rides or long walks.

She saw many doctors, going to each new one in a spirit of hope—which soon changed to despair, for none was able to arrest the increasing stiffness of her joints. But she did not allow illness to interfere with her life.

She was always aloof, even frightening to those who did not know her well: partly from shyness, reserve, and a capacity for silence which could be alarming.

Added to this was the effect of her particular kind of stately beauty. She made no concession to fashion, or to the choice of anything which would enhance it.

She showed pleasure at the presence of close friends, particularly her own family. Or if anyone was in any distress or was ill, she was all consideration, warmth and solicitude—as if it needed this to bring tenderness out of the carapace of her reserve.

Ralph was asked to write incidental music for a Cambridge production of Aristophanes' 'The Wasps' in 1909. In it he mixed the flavours of folk song with orchestral sophistication new to him.

In the chorus were two brilliant young men. One was Steuart Wilson: between him and Ralph a lifelong friendship here began.

The other was Denis Browne, who was to find immortality in company with another Cambridge man, Rupert Brooke.

A summer custom of these years was outdoor performances at Leith Hill Place of plays based on folk songs . . . Among the performers, dressed as villagers of a period that can only be described as 'Arcadian—Acting box', was Steuart Wilson.

Ralph was commissioned to write a work for the Three Choirs Festival at Gloucester in 1910.

While he had been immersed in hymns, he had used one of the nine tunes Thomas Tallis had written for Archbishop Parker's metrical Psalter of 1567 . . . He took this tune as a theme for a fantasia using strings as a solo quartet, a small string band, and a larger body of players.

The audience in the Cathedral that September evening saw Ralph stand in front of them, looking taller than ever on the high platform—dark haired, serious, inwardly extremely nervous, and the grave splendour of the 'Fantasia on a Theme by Thomas Tallis' was heard for the first time.

With the Perpendicular grandeurs of Gloucester Cathedral in mind and the strange quality of the resonance of stone, the echo ideas of three different groups of instruments was well judged. It seemed that his early love for architecture and his historical knowledge were so deeply assimilated that they were translated and absorbed into the texture and line of the music.

The 'Sea Symphony' was finished and accepted for the Leeds Festival of 1910. The Festival Choir rehearsed in Leeds, the orchestra (mostly London players) at the RCM.

Many friends came to the première on 12 October:

. . . But Ralph was scarcely aware of their presence, being completely absorbed in the terrors of his first really big work.

He had lived with the Symphony on paper for so long, and now its moment of sound had come.

He said that when the orchestra played the opening chords and the chorus came in fortissimo
    'Behold the sea itself',
he was nearly blown off the rostrum by the noise.

It was his thirty-eighth birthday.

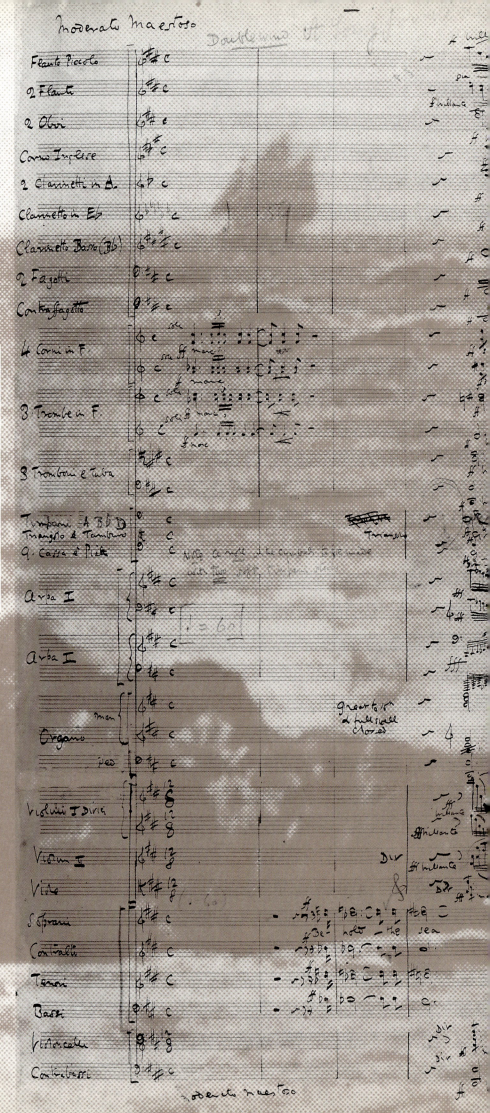

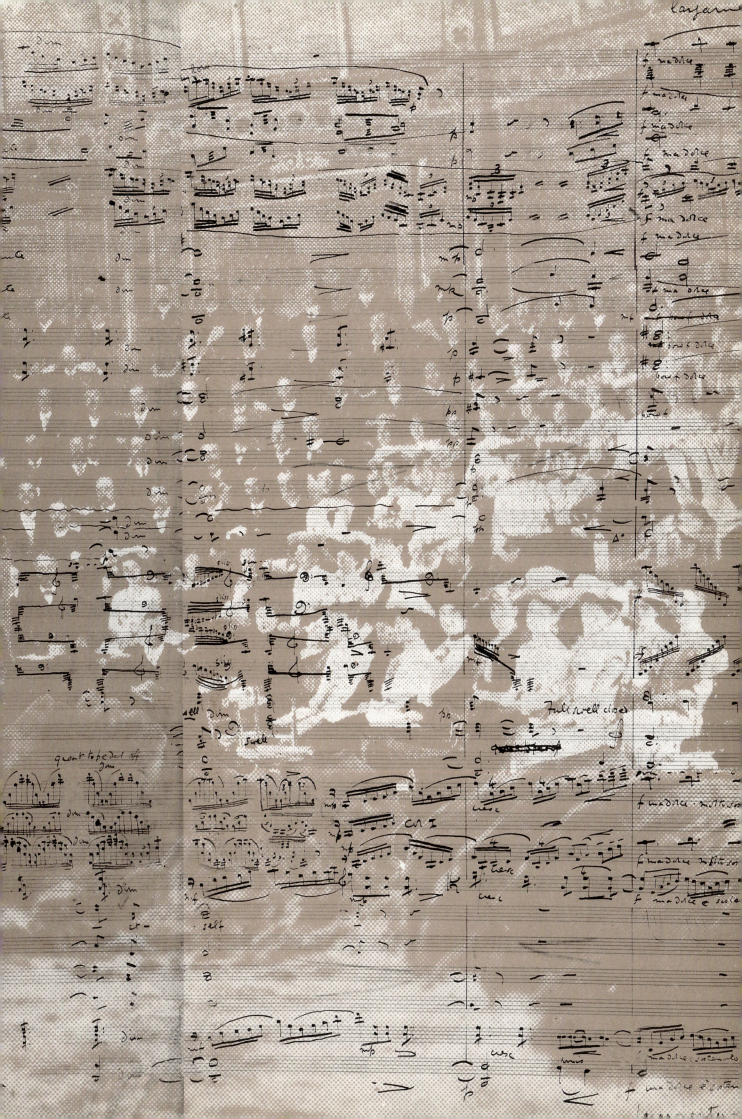

Another work of long gestation was *Five Mystical Songs*, produced at the Worcester Festival of 1911. A friend remembered seeing Ralph and Adeline in the Cathedral

. . . with the sun shining through the windows on her hair, which looked like pure gold. It was an unforgettable sight, the two of them.

He had a thick thatch of dark hair, a tall, rather heavy figure, even then slightly bowed; and his face was profoundly moving, deep humanity and yet with the quality of a mediaeval sculpture . . .

Ralph's own memory of that Festival was different . . . He had to conduct the *Five Mystical Songs première:*

'*I was thoroughly nervous. When I looked at the fiddles I thought I was going mad, for what I saw appeared to be Fritz Kreisler at a back desk.*

'*I got through somehow, and at the end I whispered to the leader, W. H. Reed, "Am I mad, or did I see Kreisler in the band?"*

'*"Oh yes," he said, "he broke a string, and wanted to play in the new one before the Elgar Concerto— and couldn't do it otherwise without being heard in the Cathedral."*'

This became one of Ralph's favourite stories, and started: '*I have done something none of the grand conductors have . . .*'

George Butterworth, a dozen years Ralph's junior, was a fine folk dancer and a composer equally dedicated to collecting folk songs. In December 1911 they made an expedition together into East Anglia.

It was Butterworth who gave the hint for the next big work. Ralph recalled:

He had been sitting with us one evening, smoking and playing: and at the end of the evening, as he was getting up to go, he said in his characteristically abrupt way:

'*You know, you ought to write a Symphony.*'

From that moment the idea of a symphony . . . dominated my mind.

When Ralph's Aunt Sophy died in November 1911, Leith Hill Place passed to Ralph's mother:

She and Meggie continued there with the same quiet dignity, the same mixture of hospitality and austerity that had hardly varied since the days of Caroline Wedgwood's widowhood in the 1870s.

Margaret Vaughan Williams at
Leith Hill Place

Ralph accepted a commission to arrange and conduct music for Sir Frank Benson's Shakespeare season at Stratford-upon-Avon early in 1913. The plays included 'Richard II' and 'The Merry Wives of Windsor'.
He sat up all one night orchestrating 'Greensleeves' and copying parts for the next day's performance.
It sowed the seed for an opera about Falstaff.

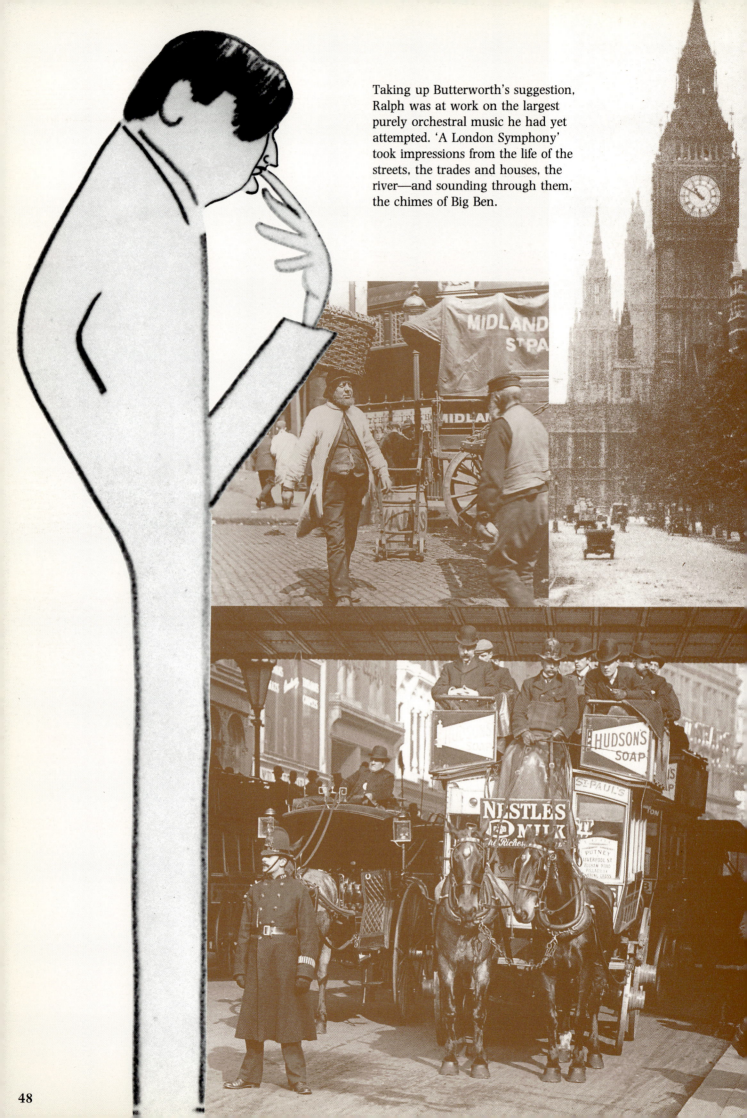

Taking up Butterworth's suggestion,
Ralph was at work on the largest
purely orchestral music he had yet
attempted. 'A London Symphony'
took impressions from the life of the
streets, the trades and houses, the
river—and sounding through them,
the chimes of Big Ben.

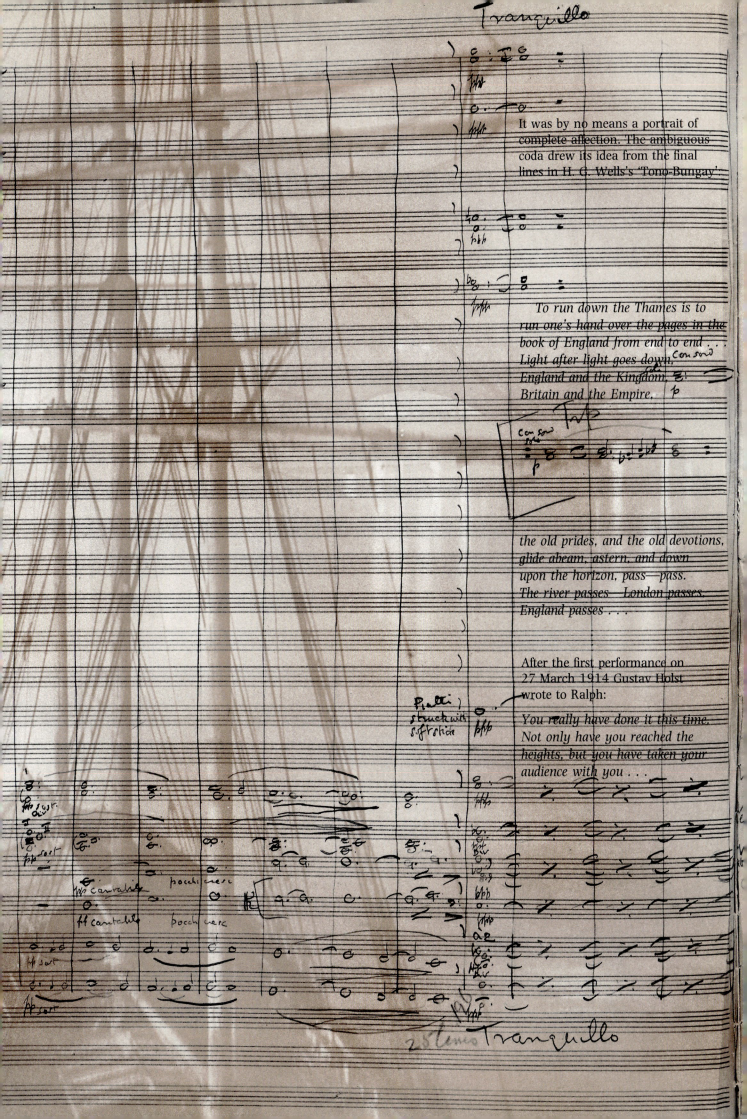

Tranquillo

It was by no means a portrait of
complete affection. The ambiguous
coda drew its idea from the final
lines in H. G. Wells's 'Tono-Bungay'

To run down the Thames is to
run one's hand over the pages in the
book of England from end to end . . .
Light after light goes down.
England and the Kingdom,
Britain and the Empire,

the old prides, and the old devotions,
glide abeam, astern, and down
upon the horizon, pass—pass.
The river passes—London passes,
England passes . . .

After the first performance on
27 March 1914 Gustav Holst
wrote to Ralph:

You really have done it this time.
Not only have you reached the
heights, but you have taken your
audience with you . . .

Two other works had been slowly evolving. One was an extended pastoral for violin and orchestra on Meredith's poem, 'The Lark Ascending'. The other was his first mature opera, *Hugh the Drover*. Then everything was interrupted by the declaration of war on 4 August 1914.

On 5 August, the day after war was declared, Ralph and Adeline left London to stay at Margate . . .

Ralph, walking on the cliffs looking over the Channel, where the B.E.F. were already crossing towards the battlefields, sat down to write a tune he had thought of and grew absorbed in his music notebook.

He was recalled to time and place by a small Boy Scout who gazed at him fiercely and told him that he was under arrest.

'Why?' asked Ralph, puzzled.

'Maps,' said the scout. 'Information for the enemy.'

Feeling rather like Hugh the Drover accused of spying for Boney, Ralph allowed himself to be escorted to the police station, showed his suspicious MS paper, and was let off with a caution.

By the time Ralph and Adeline returned to London, many younger friends had enlisted—Butterworth, R. O. Morris (who was soon to marry Adeline's sister Emmy), Geoffrey Toye (who had conducted the 'London Symphony' première), F. B. Ellis (who had shared the conducting that night).

Ralph, now nearly forty-two, joined the Special Constabulary, formed to replace policemen called up. It was not enough.

In a few weeks he volunteered for the Army Medical Corps. For the remainder of 1914, he was training in London and able to live at home in Cheyne Walk.

Ralph hated the war . . . He knew that he could have stayed in England. He knew also that if he did so, he would not be able to write: he would be burdened with a sense of evading his responsibility as a man, his duty as a citizen.

Ralph (*left*) with RAMC working party.

On January 1 1915 the unit was moved to Dorking, and billeted there to continue their training.

There were no wagons and no horses, so the wagon orderlies had to take part in route marches, sometimes to Guildford and back.

Ralph's habit of long walks made it possible for him to manage, but those days of marching called on all his powers of endurance and fortitude.

While Ralph was stationed at Dorking, it was easy for him to go home for short periods of leave—or for Adeline to visit him, which she did constantly.

The unit moved to Saffron Walden, and then to Salisbury Plain for the first half of 1916.

Much older than most of his fellows, unused to the order expected at kit inspections, finding difficulty in wearing uniform correctly, in putting his puttees on straight, and wearing his cap at the correct angle, and in many other details of daily life, he found these minor afflictions called for elementary skills he had never before needed and had not got.

His cheerful acceptance of difficulties, and his willingness to do everything that much younger men could do more easily, impressed his comrades. Among them Harry Steggles . . . his junior by more than twenty years, became his particular support. Their friendship had started with Ralph's interest in the fact that Harry played a mouth organ with real musicianship, and on the other side with

Harry's protective help in looking after equipment. It became an affectionate partnership shared throughout Ralph's career in the Ambulance. Harry called him Bob, and treated him as both elder and younger brother.

Summer 1916 on Salisbury Plain. In the row standing, Harry Steggles is on the left and Ralph next to him.

Ralph wrote to Gustav Holst (who had dropped the 'von' from his name):

I am 'waggon orderly' and go up the line every night to bring back wounded and sick in a motor ambulance . . .
I sometimes dread coming back to life with so many gaps—

especially of course George Butterworth [killed in action 5 August]—he has left most of his MS to me—and now I hear that Ellis is killed. Out of those seven who joined up together in August 1914, only three are left.

Field Ambulance on the Somme, 1916: stretcher cases by the roadside awaiting transport to base hospitals.

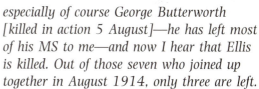

In the midst of it all, musical ideas were slowly gathering toward what would become 'A Pastoral Symphony':

It's really war-time music—a great deal of it incubated when I used to go up night after night with the ambulance waggon at Ecoivres and we went up a steep hill and there was a wonderful Corot-like landscape in the sunset.

Late in 1916 Ralph's unit was sent to Salonika:
there was little to do and he was restless.
  He was able to return to England to be trained
for a commission in the Royal Garrison Artillery.
  In March 1918 he returned to France as a
subaltern on active service with the Artillery.

The tremendous reports over weeks and months damaged the hearing of many gunners.

The legacy of Ralph's Artillery service was to come in gradually increasing deafness through his later years.

After the Armistice in November 1918, Ralph was made Director of Music of the 1st Army BEF before being demobilized in February 1919.

Return was not a simple and joyful release. He was going back to a world that lacked many of his friends . . . He was also going back to discover how his own invention had survived the years of suppression . . .

He revised the 'London Symphony', which now bore a dedication 'To the memory of George Butterworth'.

He finished an extended romance for violin and orchestra, almost completed in 1914. *The Lark Ascending* took its inspiration from the poem by George Meredith:

> *'He rises and begins to round,*
> *He drops the silver chain of sound . . .*
> *For singing till his heaven fills,*
> *'Tis love of earth that he instils . . .*
> *Till lost on his aerial rings*
> *In light, and then the fancy sings.'*

'The Skylark', etching by Samuel Palmer

At the Royal College of Music, the new Director (following the death of Parry) was Hugh Allen. He invited Ralph to teach composition.

Joining the staff at the R.C.M. was the beginning of more than twenty years of work there.

Ralph found it interesting, though he said that he was not a good teacher . . . One of his pupils, Elizabeth Maconchy, has written: '. . . he had worked out his own salvation as a composer, and he encouraged his pupils to do the same.'

Among his pupils in the first years were some, like himself, recently demobilized, Patrick Hadley and Ivor Gurney.

Others included Gustav Holst's daughter Imogen, and Gordon Jacob (who wrote of Ralph):

He was an instinctive poet in music, and at that time had an instinctive horror of professional skill and technical ability.

As he grew older, he came to realize that these qualities did not necessarily add up to superficial slickness, and his later pupils were put through the mill.

Before the war ended, Adeline had shut up their home in Chelsea and had moved to furnished rooms at Sheringham in Norfolk, to look after her ill brother Hervey. Until Hervey died in May 1921, much of Ralph's time was spent at Sheringham.

At last, more than two years after his return from the war, they could settle down once again in Cheyne Walk, Chelsea.

In the spring of 1921 he directed the first post-war Leith Hill Festival.

He also accepted conductorship of the London Bach Choir. With them he was soon to direct his first *St. Matthew Passion*.

His formative years in Victorian and Edwardian England had been cast in distant shadows by the horror and nullity of the war.

The most important task for his art now was finding ways to reconcile the contradictions. He found some of his reconciliation through the compassionate elegy of 'A Pastoral Symphony'.

The road from Ypres after the Armistice.

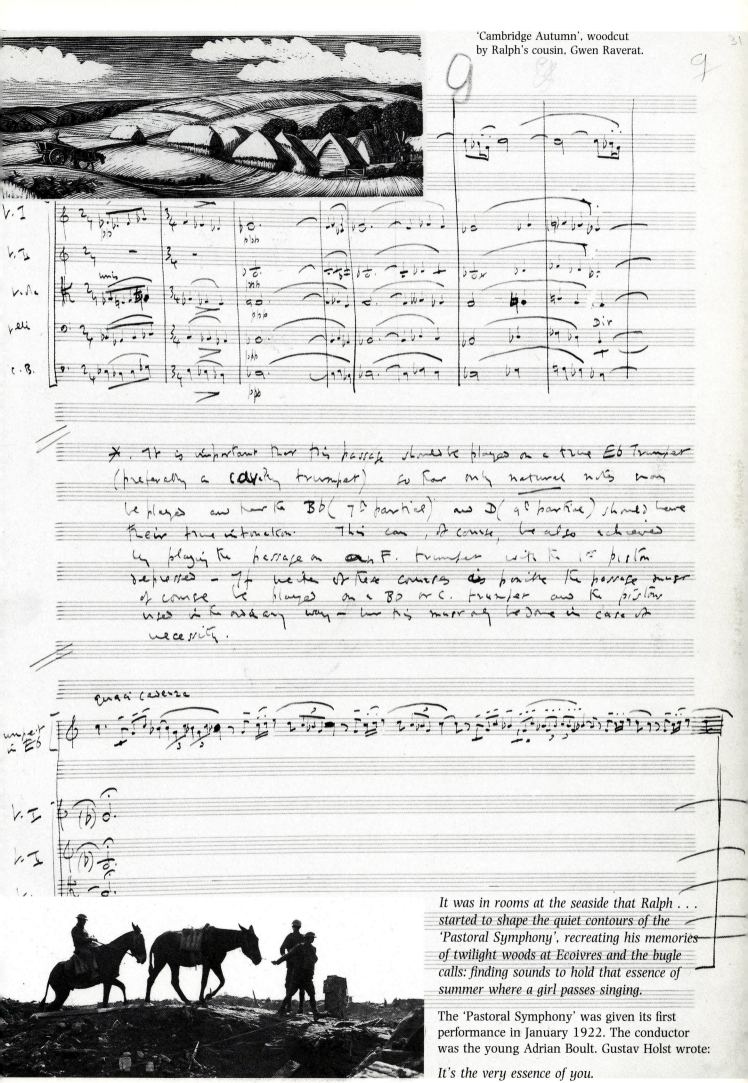

'Cambridge Autumn', woodcut
by Ralph's cousin, Gwen Raverat.

It was in rooms at the seaside that Ralph . . .
started to shape the quiet contours of the
'Pastoral Symphony', recreating his memories
of twilight woods at Ecoivres and the bugle
calls: finding sounds to hold that essence of
summer where a girl passes singing.

The 'Pastoral Symphony' was given its first
performance in January 1922. The conductor
was the young Adrian Boult. Gustav Holst wrote:

It's the very essence of you.

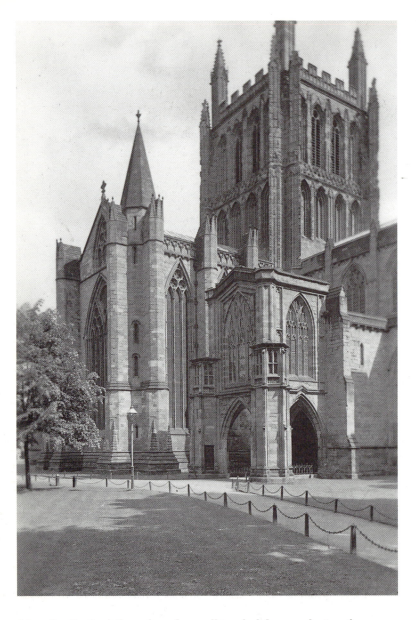

Ralph's friendship with Gustav Holst was now more than a quarter century old. Holst's 'Hymn of Jesus' was dedicated to Ralph.

At the Hereford Festival in September 1921, Gustav conducted the 'Hymn of Jesus' and Ralph his 'Tallis Fantasia'.

After the Festival they shared a walking holiday, exploring the Malvern Hills east of Hereford.

The usual plan for these holidays was a twelve or fifteen mile walk a day—time to enjoy the country, with stops to revive Ralph . . . by a rest and a glass of beer, or a good farmhouse tea.

It was still almost the world Borrow had known . . . Green roads, deep lanes, and footpaths took walkers into countryside where farms were rarely mechanized, and stooks were still the graceful tented shapes of Samuel Palmer's landscapes.

During 1921 Ralph had been at work on a Mass. He said cheerfully:

There is no reason why an atheist could not write a good Mass.
The Mass in G minor was published in 1922 with a dedication
To Gustav Holst and his Whitsuntide Singers.

The Whitsuntide Singers
with Gustav (*left*) and Ralph (*right*)
outside Chichester Cathedral
before their performance of the Mass

In May 1922 Ralph and Adeline went for their first visit to the United States. An invitation had come from the wealthy Carl Stoeckel to conduct the first American performance of the 'Pastoral Symphony' at the festival in Norfolk, Connecticut.

Shipboard acquaintances: (left to right) R. T. Paté, Miss Tait, the comedian Will Fyffe, and Ralph.

The visit began in New York. Ralph wrote to Gustav Holst from the Plaza Hotel:

My millionaire has put us up at the swaggerest hotel in N.Y. . . . We were whirled off in a taxi and up 16 floors in an elevator—to a suite of rooms with 2 bathrooms and this wonderful view all over N.Y. . . .

I have seen (a) Niagara, (b) the Woolworth buildings and am most impressed by (b). I've come to the conclusion that the Works of Man terrify me more than the Works of God.

They had seen white New England villages, Ralph had been excited by names familiar from Whitman's poems, as well as by the towers and chasms of New York.

During work on the 'Pastoral Symphony', he had made a further setting from Bunyan's *Pilgrim's Progress*—an opera named *The Shepherds of the Delectable Mountains*.

Ralph and Adeline returned from New York in time for its first performance at the Royal College of Music in July 1922.

A professional production of *The Shepherds of the Delectable Mountains* at Sadler's Wells in 1947

Side by side with the Folk Song Society, Ralph's friend Cecil Sharp had founded the English Folk Dance Society.

Ralph was president of the Cambridge branch. They asked him to write a ballet incorporating folk tunes and dances. It offered a first real venture into the world of dance.

The result was *Old King Cole*, designed for performance in Nevile's Court, Trinity College in May 1923.

The scenario was an entertainment devised by the King for his daughter Helena, married to the Roman Emperor but back for a visit.

Three native fiddlers played in succession—the first a gypsy Morris jig, the second a romantic rendering of 'A bold young farmer', the third a jolly Sword Dance. The third was the King's choice for the prize.

But after the company had gone in to supper, Helena lingered behind to catch the last strains of the second fiddler, throwing a rose after him as he wandered away through the darkened court.

Conversing with a Morris Dancer

The choreographer of *Old King Cole* was another EFDS member, Mrs Burnaby. She recalled:

The two processions entered on each side along the cloisters, and Old King Cole came on through the Hall door on to the Tribune—Exeunt at the end through that door into the Hall for the banquet! The second fiddler going off alone to the right down the cloister.

Hugh the Drover (much of it laid out before the war) was the result of Ralph's wish to write a 'musical' about old English country life—'real as far as possible—not sham'. Some of it was based on folk songs.

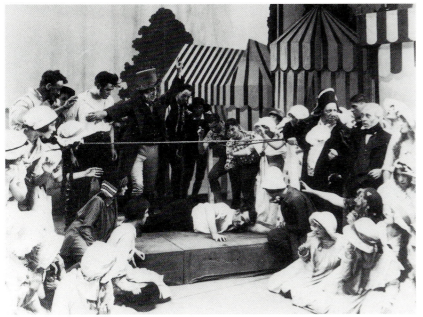

Hugh the Drover achieved two productions in July 1924—one at the RCM, the other by the British National Opera Company under Malcolm Sargent.

Ralph wanted the sound of bells chiming a tune—as they do at Northleach in Gloucestershire (which was the sort of village in which he imagined the story to be set) . . .

So he liked the idea of the village church being part of the set.

But he was greatly surprised when Queen Mary (who came to the performance, and to whom he was presented), asked him why hero and heroine had not used it to be married in before they set off for the open road.

Hugh was to keep Ralph's attention for the rest of his life. He returned to it again and again—taking out a section here, reworking or adding a song there. The last revision came in 1956, nearly half a century after the opera's beginning.

At the Norwich Festival of 1924, Ralph conducted the 'Sea Symphony'.

After it was over, Queen Mary, who had been in the audience, sent for him.

He was fetched from his dressing-room, protesting that he was not fit to be seen. 'Go and tell her my collar has collapsed completely,' he said to the messenger.

'She knows—come along.'

He tried again: 'Tell her I'm an awful man—with seventeen wives.' He thought of 'Hugh', and wondered what he had left undone this time.

'Oh, she knows all that,' and the messenger hustled him into the Royal presence. But this time it was for congratulations on the work and its performance.

In 1924 the Oxford University Press established a Music Department under the direction of Hubert Foss, who was himself a musician. He had imagination, a scholarly mind, great understanding, and—when necessary—courage.

As far as Ralph was concerned he found that

'Ask Foss's advice'—

'Ask Foss to see it'—

'Ask Foss to play it over to me at Amen House' became almost daily sayings. In him Ralph found the ideal publisher.

One of Ralph's first publications with Oxford University Press was his next work, *Flos Campi.*

Flos Campi ('I am the Rose of Sharon, and the Lily of the Valleys') was the most sensuous work Ralph ever wrote. Each of its six sections is prefaced by printed words from 'The Song of Songs': the six in sequence evoke the whole act of love.

A solo viola sings the wordless song of the lover, answered by a wordless chorus with melodies that say all, within a rich orchestral setting.

Adeline, Gustav Holst, and his assistants at St Paul's School, Nora Day and Vally Lasker (skilled pianists who often helped Ralph by trying over projected music), with Ralph and his old friend Dorothy Longman

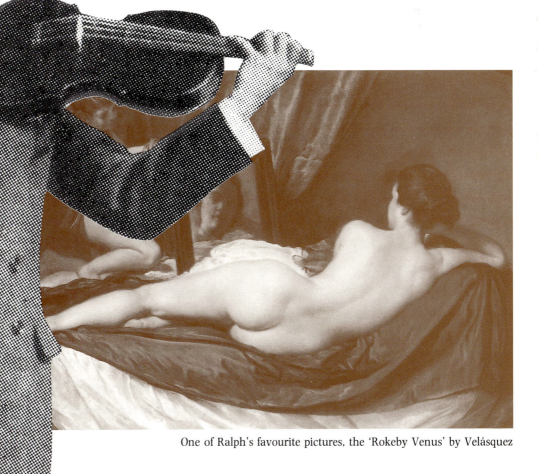

One of Ralph's favourite pictures, the 'Rokeby Venus' by Velásquez

The first performance of *Flos Campi*, with the violist Lionel Tertis, was planned for October 1925. Rehearsing for it, the orchestral players—many veterans of the War and none of them missing the significance of the music—wickedly dubbed it 'Camp Flossie'. That delighted Ralph.

But Gustav Holst wrote to him: 'I couldn't get hold of Flos a bit and was therefore disappointed with it and me.'

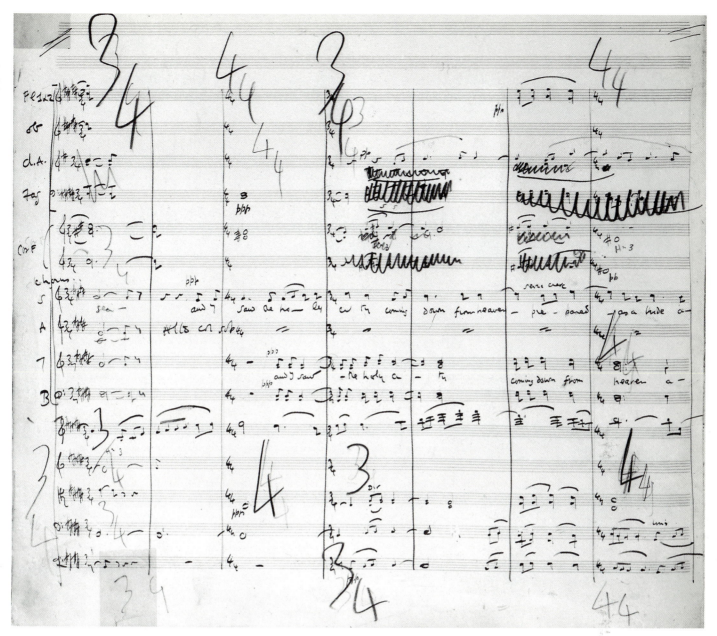

An obverse image of *Flos Campi* emerged in Ralph's next work. It was a short oratorio, *Sancta Civitas*.

The Text, largely from the Book of Revelation, described the conflict of Earth and Heaven. Then:

. . . I saw the holy city coming down from heaven, prepared as a bride adorned for her husband, having the glory of God.

Around the time he had begun work on *Sancta Civitas*, Ralph had written:

The human, visible, audible and intelligible media which artists (of all kinds) use, are symbols . . . of what lies beyond sense and knowledge.

Illumination of Gloucester Cathedral reflected on clouds

Ralph still had the old family *Shakespeare* which he had known from childhood. There he had first encountered 'The Merry Wives of Windsor' and 'Greensleeves'.

Since his music for the Stratford production of 1913, the notion of an opera had been in his mind. At first he called it 'The Fat Knight': but soon he found the title for the story he wanted to tell—'Sir John in Love'.

'Greensleeves' and other favourite folk tunes were embedded in the score, matched by his own affectionate melodies.

He wrote *Sir John in Love* over several years. It was produced at the Royal College of Music in 1929.

Side by side with *Sir John in Love* he worked at a romantic extravaganza, *The Poisoned Kiss*.

Sir John in Love had formed a complement to Holst's *At the Boar's Head*.
But Ralph did not show *The Poisoned Kiss* to Gustav.

Early in October 1927 Adeline had a fall and broke her thigh so badly that she was encased in plaster from chest to toes. . . .

Ralph and Adeline came to the conclusion that they must leave the tall house in Cheyne Walk, and find somewhere to live that would be easier for her. . . .

She longed for the country, so they decided to spend a summer near Dorking and look for a house.

It was the summer of 1929 before they found 'The White Gates'.

The house stood in a lane leading out of the main Guildford road, with fields at the other end. It had a garden with flowering trees, an orchard, and a tennis court . . .

Looking east, the ridge rises beyond the town and St Martin's Church to Box Hill and the sweeping curve of the Downs.

At Dorking Adeline went through the process of learning to walk again. But her arthritis steadily worsened.

With the help of a crutch, she was still able to walk in the garden.

She was very thin. The cool beauty of her youth had changed to gaunt and austere age.

Her back was straight, her head beautifully set on her shoulders, and her heavy eyelids in their deep sockets lifted to show pale blue eyes—where amusement could flash or fury blaze, though she usually looked at the world with gently irony.

Pain had taught her stillness, and she had a quality of heroic endurance that could be intimidating. . . .

She often preferred to go to rehearsals rather than performances, especially if the performances were broadcast and she could listen at home.

Ralph's study, facing west and south, had a french window opening into the garden . . . In this he had a large kitchen table on which music accumulated, as it did on the window seat . . .

Here he installed his little upright piano, wall bookcases brought from Cheyne Walk, a writing desk, and a huge arm-chair.

R. O. Morris's niece, Honorine Williamson, had come to help Adeline in the house. She settled into the household as a much-loved niece, friend, and ally for the next twelve years. . . .

They had a car which Honorine drove.

Ralph realized just how much more bother it was going to be . . . for him to enjoy from Dorking the musical life he had had for the past thirty years. . . .

He had long felt himself essentially a Londoner, and he never ceased to miss the town life—the pleasure of wandering into the Tate Gallery for an hour, the river in front of his window, and most of all the Bach Choir rehearsals.

He resigned the Bach Choir conductorship, as journeys to rehearsals would take too much time on top of his teaching at the RCM.

The works of William Blake were collected by Geoffrey Keynes. He was a brother-in-law of Gwen Raverat, and thus a member of the Cambridge 'family'. He recalled:

In 1927 my balletomania and admiration for the works of William Blake suddenly coalesced. I had recently acquired Blake's 'Illustrations of the Book of Job' . . . It came to me that the groupings and gestures of the figures were asking to be put into actual motion on stage . . .

My first appeal was to Gwen Raverat . . . We had long discussions on the most suitable composer and finally chose Dr. Ralph Vaughan Williams . . .

He was immediately struck with the possibilities, and was soon so fired with enthusiasm that he became rather difficult to control.

He expressed, however, a great dislike of dancing 'on points' (an essential feature of classical ballet) which made him feel ill. We agreed there should be none of this, and to his calling the production 'A Masque for Dancing' . . .

In July 1931 *Job* was mounted on the stage of the Cambridge Theatre, London. The sets and costumes were by Gwen Raverat, with choreography by Ninette de Valois, and Ralph's lavish orchestration reduced to theatre pit size by Constant Lambert.

The role of Satan was danced by Anton Dolin

Ongoing projects enlarged the darkness in *Job*. One was a short opera setting Synge's *Riders to the Sea*. Begun in 1925, its composition extended over the next decade. It was to be the most powerfully concentrated of all Ralph's operas.

In a lonely cottage by the sea, the singers are pitted against an ever-present orchestral menace of the sea without. It was a mirror reversal of the visionary 'Sea Symphony' conceived in the antediluvian years before the Great War.

Even after publication in 1936, *Riders to the Sea* would have to wait for a performance. Full stage productions, like that at the RCM in 1969 (*below*) have been rare.

Over both *Riders to the Sea* and a new Symphony. Ralph had much-valued 'field days' of consultation with his beloved friend of thirty-five years, Gustav Holst.

The Fourth Symphony, begun in 1931, distilled grimness and violence in the orchestra. Finishing it three years later, Ralph reflected:

I wrote it not as a definite picture of anything external—e.g. the state of Europe—but simply because it occurred to me like this . . .

One friend, Elizabeth Trevelyan, wrote:

I found your poisonous temper in the Scherzo contrasted with that rollicking lovely opening of the Trio . . .

1934 changed everything in English music. Elgar (with whom Ralph had formed a late affectionate friendship) died in February. Delius followed in June. But the death which hit Ralph hardest was that of Gustav Holst on 25 May:

My only thought is now which ever way I turn, what are we to do without him— everything seems to have turned back to him— what would Gustav think or advise or do—

During a conversation in 1932, Elgar had suggested making an oratorio out of 'Elinor Rumming'—the beer-brewing hag in the early Tudor verse of John Skelton:

Droopy and drowsy,
Scurvy and lowsy,
Her face all bowsy . . .

and so on for hundreds of lines.
'Pure jazz' was Elgar's characterization.
Ralph read a newly printed edition of Skelton, and found four more 'Tudor Portraits' to add.

Elinor Rumming

'My pretty Bess. Turn once again to me!' sung by a swain

Ralph conducted the première of Five Tudor Portraits at the Norwich Festival in September 1936.
The programme was to be shared with the première of Our Hunting Fathers by the twenty-two year old Benjamin Britten. The soprano soloist, Sophie Wyss, recalled Ralph at a rehearsal:

The orchestra behaved like naughty schoolboys, not understanding Britten's musical idiom. Dr Vaughan Williams was at the rehearsal and reproved them, and they pulled themselves together and gave a fair performance.
I will remember him not only as the great composer he was, but as the champion of fair play.

John Jayberd: burlesque epitaph
on a troublesome parish clerk

Jane Scroop's lament for Philip
Sparrow, killed by a cat

Jolly Rutterkin

The Order of Merit was conferred on Ralph in the Silver Jubilee Honours
of 1935. Thus the King, with the musical nation clearly behind him,
acknowledged Ralph as head of the profession in England.

At a celebration with friends, Ralph was snapped with his brother
Hervey (who now occupied their childhood home, Leith Hill Place).

*Ralph had reached what must have seemed the peak of his life. His
music was widely known. His fellow musicians knew he was a man to
whom they could turn when authority was needed in any cause.*

*He had many friends, a comfortable income augmented now by
royalties, and (except for a liability to catch cold) his health was
excellent.*

*Most important, he had an unending flow of musical thought and
invention. His work absorbed him and, because he taught and conducted
and went to as many concerts as possible, he had the constant
stimulation of exploring the works of other composers, including those of
his own students.*

*His life at home was shared with a wife devoted to him, whose
interest in his music had grown deeper, more critical and more helpful
through the years . . . In spite of her arthritis, Adeline was still able to
go about in their car . . .*

*She was devoted to Ralph's mother—who, with her maid and her
little dog, spent most of the year at 'The White Gates', and who still
looked on her son and daughter-in-law as her 'dear children'.*

By the middle 1930s the clouds of menace possessed a definite shape. Much of 1935 was devoted to writing *Dona Nobis Pacem*. Beginning with the Latin prayer, the words Ralph chose moved through violence to a Biblical vision of peace among nations.

At the centre of the new work was an old setting never until now published: Walt Whitman's 'Dirge for Two Veterans'. Its appearance here gained special poignancy from the fame these words had already acquired in the setting by Gustav Holst.

Ralph had written no funeral music for Gustav: that was not his way. But the placement of this old yet heretofore unknown setting of his own at the centre of impassioned exhortation now made of it a reflecting crystal.

Ralph and Gustav had been two veterans, and the Dirge was for their friendship. Whitman's veterans were father and son: Gustav had been the younger, but he was (in Ralph's generous mind) godfather to some of his friend's biggest music.

At the time of finishing *Dona Nobis Pacem*, Ralph recalled something Gustav had said to him:

'The artist is born again and starts again with every fresh work—'.

'The Sleeping Shepherd' by Samuel Palmer

whir - ring And ev-e-ry blow of the great con-vul-sive drums_ strike me through and
whir - ring And ev-e-ry blow of the great con-vul-sive drums_ strike me through and
whir - ring And ev-e-ry blow of the great con-vul-sive drums_ strike me through and
whir - ring And ev-e-ry blow of the great con-vul-sive drums_ strike me through and

For the Coronation of King George VI and Queen Elizabeth in May 1937, Ralph wrote an orchestral 'Flourish' and the Te Deum for the service in Westminster Abbey.

In November 1937 Ralph's mother died. Margaret Vaughan Williams was ninety-five. She had been a widow for sixty-two years, and had outlived her daughter Meggie by six years.

Her life had bridged so many changes, so much history, and she had watched it all with alert and informed interest. She belonged to a very different world from Ralph's. Frances Cornford (observing from a family vantage point) saw 'the deeply evangelical austerity against which Ralph revolted with passion', as well as the serenity, hospitality, and grace of her life.

Ralph was starting another symphony—using music that had been accumulating for a full scale opera on *The Pilgrim's Progress*, which he felt he would never finish.

At that moment he met the twenty-seven year old Ursula Wood, who recalled:

I had seen 'Job' in the 1932–33 season while I was a student at the Old Vic. Before this I had heard very little music, and had not much enjoyed what I had heard. Visually 'Job' was familiar, for I knew the Blake illustrations; but the music was a new world, and I was completely overcome by it.

For the next five years I thought of writing to the composer, though I never made any particular effort to hear any of his other works. This was partly because, after that glorious break away into the different world of the Old Vic, I had returned to army life—in which I had been brought up, and into which I married. My husband, Michael Wood, was at that time a Gunnery Instructor, and our life was nomadic.

By 1937 I had written a ballet scenario . . . and I screwed up enough courage to send it to Dr. Vaughan Williams. . . . So on 31 March 1938 we met.
I do not know which of us was the more surprised. He had, it seemed, expected a sensible matron in sensible shoes. I had not expected someone so large and so beautiful.
. . . At that meeting we talked mostly about poetry . . . and we ended up sitting by the Serpentine and talking about madrigal poems.

Soon they were collaborating over a masque founded on Spenser's 'Epithalamion'. Its title was *The Bridal Day*. At his request, she gave him this photograph.

Sir Henry Wood was to celebrate his golden jubilee as a conductor. He asked Ralph for work to include sixteen favourite singers with orchestra. Ralph chose a passage from 'The Merchant of Venice'. He told Ursula Wood (no relation to Sir Henry):

'I've always wanted to set the Jessica and Lorenzo scene . . .'
'Eight Jessicas and eight Lorenzos?' I asked.
'No, just a little bit for each voice.'
And so the 'Serenade to Music' was written.

Ralph and Sir Henry Wood (centre) with the sixteen singers at Abbey Road Studios to record the *Serenade to Music* a few days after the première in October 1938

Two Surrey pageants were devised by Ralph and E. M. Forster. For the first, at Abinger in 1934, they met on the ground to plan it. When Ralph saw the photograph above, he said:

I look like a rich and wily cattle-dealer getting round a simple rustic.

The second Pageant was entitled 'England's Pleasant Land'. It contained sketches of the new 'Pilgrim's Progress' symphony 'as a try-out'.

Ralph conducted a performance at Milton Court on 9 July 1938.

Early in 1938 Ralph had received the offer of a prize from the University of Hamburg. He responded:

. . . I am strongly opposed to the present system of government in Germany, especially with regard to its treatment of artists and scholars . . . and my first instinct is to refuse . . .

You have assured me that this honour is offered purely in the cause of art by a learned body to a member of the English musical profession; that it implies no political propaganda; and that I shall feel free as an honourable man, if I accept, to hold and express any views on the general state of Germany which are allowable to any British citizen.

In these circumstances I have pleasure in cordially accepting the honour.

Within eight months Ralph's music was on Hitler's black list.

Die

hanſiſche Univerſität zu hamburg

verleiht den

hanſiſchen Shakeſpeare-Preis

für das Jahr 1937

Dr. Ralph Vaughan Williams,

der auf allen Gebieten des muſikaliſchen Schaffens in Liedern, Chorwerken und Opern, in Kammer-muſiken und Symphonien als ſchöpferiſcher Meiſter hervorgetreten iſt,

der, von Volkslied und Volkstanz ausgehend, die altengliſchen Volksweiſen zur Grundlage ſeines eigenen Stils gemacht hat,

der damit die natürliche Verbindung zur großen Überlieferung der Eliſabethaniſchen Muſik, deren Nährboden auch das Volkslied geweſen iſt, wieder-hergeſtellt hat,

der ein Bahnbrecher für die Erneuerung einer national gerichteten Kunſt iſt in der Überzeugung, daß jedes Volk durch die Entfaltung ſeiner eigenen Art den wertvollſten Beitrag zum Ganzen der europäiſchen Kultur leiſtet.

hamburg, am 15. Juni 1938

Der Rektor der hanſiſchen Univerſität

Adolf Rein

The Dorking Committee for Refugees from Nazi oppression started work in December 1938. Ralph was naturally one of the first people asked to join, and he took a full share of work.

On 3 September 1939 Britain entered the Second World War. Ursula Wood was to recall those days:

The beginning of the war made Ralph feel desperate for useful work. He immediately offered the use of his field to the District Council for allotments, reserving a patch for himself . . .

He was one of the small committee who worked to put into practice Myra Hess's idea of lunch-time concerts in the National Gallery . . .

He wrote to me at the end of September 1939:

'Is it Herbert Fisher's "History of Europe" you are reading—magnificent but depressing—all good things men try to do perish . . .'.

Looking for some way to make his music serve the country in war-time, Ralph asked about writing for films. The result was an invitation from his former pupil Muir Mathieson (now musical director for London Films) to do the score for a spy adventure, *49th Parallel*.

'How long can I have?' asked Ralph.
'Till Wednesday.'

In a witty essay, 'Composing for the Films', written a few years later, Ralph summarized his discovery that the best way to write film music

. . . is to ignore the details and to intensify the spirit of the whole situation by a continuous stream of music. This stream can be modified (often at rehearsal!) by points of colour superimposed on the flow.

For example, your music is illustrating Columbus's voyage and you have a sombre tune symbolizing the weariness of the voyage, the depression of the crew, and the doubts of Columbus.

But the producer says: 'I want a little bit of sunshine music for that flash on the waves.'

If you are wise, you will send the orchestra away for five minutes, which will delight them. Then you look at the score to find out what instruments are unemployed —say, the harp and two muted trumpets. You write in your sunlight at the appropriate second. You recall the orchestra. You then play the altered version, while the producer marvels at your skill in composing what appears to him to be an entirely new piece of music in so short a time.

49th Parallel, with Leslie Howard (right)

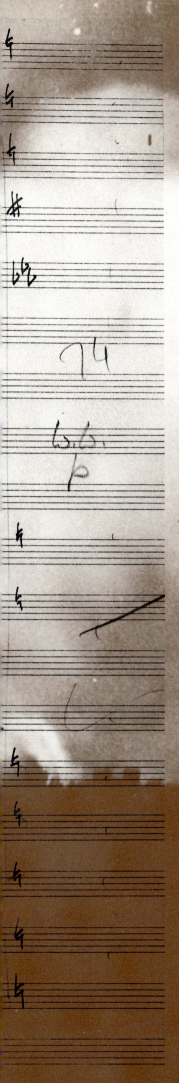

The Battle of Britain in 1940 was the worst time. Then American help began to come.

In October 1942 Ralph was seventy. 'Randolph' Wedgwood wrote:

The last Rembrandts were the best, the last Titians the most surprising—the arts often give to old age its finest moments, those which look forward over the edge of the world which surrounds them into the future. Go forward and prosper . . .

Early in 1943 Ralph finished the Symphony based partly on *Pilgrim's Progress* material. It was his Fifth.

He arranged a two-piano play-through. Adeline was well enough to come, and they were joined by Ursula, who wrote:

I had never heard this sort of thing before . . . but I watched Ralph's concentration and saw how much he was getting out of the play-through.

He conducted the first performance at an Albert Hall Prom on 24 June 1943. Ursula wrote:

There was an air raid that night—which seemed irrelevant. The Symphony's majestic vision came, at that moment, as balm to the spirit.

The new work received the greatest acclaim of any Symphony he had yet written.

Returning from the play-through of the Fifth Symphony, Adeline had had another fall. After that she never walked again. Yet she continued to help Ralph in various ways. Their process of dealing with post was observed by Ursula Wood:

. . . Ralph with a pile of letters on his knees, Adeline in her tall wheeled chair with a stiff board and writing paper on her knee. Her hands were bent with arthritis, and her hold on the pen looked precarious. But she would write at great speed, and her flowing hand was legible as well as distinctive.

In 1942 Ursula's husband Michael Wood died very suddenly while on Army service. When the telegram came, Ralph happened to be with her. Instantly he brought her back to 'The White Gates':

I stayed for a week, and Ralph took me to tea with his brother Hervey at Leith Hill Place, where the azaleas were in full flower.

Soon afterwards Ursula's plans were interrupted by a foot injury. She was invited back to 'The White Gates' to recuperate:

It was then that I found I had become part of their lives. Adeline was approachable because disaster and mis-adventure brought her warmest feelings to the surface.

Ralph, to my infinite surprise, suggested I should bring my writing into the study while he worked, and cleared a patch on one of his tables for me. I sat in the window seat, he at his desk—dashing to the piano every now and then, or stopping to say something about anything in the world —from weather for gardening to a curious technical point about film music . . .

So the summer settled into a time of content, and far more than seemed possible was salvaged.

In May 1944 Ralph's elder brother Hervey died. He had lived for many years at Leith Hill Place: and he left the house with all its land to Ralph. Ursula recalled:

. . . Ralph spent a day by himself walking through the woods, looking at the farm, the cottages, the great kitchen garden and all the orchards, fields, and the woods in flower with azaleas and bluebells, asking himself whether he wanted to return to live there.

He said to me: 'If I had to decide what trees were to be cut, what vegetables planted, what cows sold, I should lose all pleasure in the place—and if I ran the place properly I shouldn't have any time for my own work.'

Ralph made up his mind to give Leith Hill Place to the National Trust. He went there to meet James Lees-Milne, who wrote in his diary:

9 June 1944. The composer is a very sweet man, with a most impressive appearance. He is big and broad and has a large head with sharply defined features, and eyes that look far into the distance. . . . In the car he told me that when young musicians came to him for advice he always discouraged them, for he said that those who seriously

intended to make music their career would always do so willy-nilly. He has a quiet, dry humour which expresses itself in very few words. He laughs in a low key.

By the best of fortune, the National Trust's tenant at Leith Hill Place was Ralph's cousin and friend from Cambridge days, 'Randolph' Wedgwood. The renewal of this old friendship—made easy by proximity and lovely by the way Randolph's wife redecorated the house—was immensely important to Ralph.

BLACKHEATH BROCKHAM CAPEL FETCHAM SHALFORD
DORKING HOLMBURY HEADLEY FOREST GREEN WESTCOTT
HORSLEY MICKLEHAM BANSTEAD BETCHWORTH EWELL
OXSHOTT ALBURY BOOKHAM LEATHERHEAD EPSOM
BUCKLAND WARNHAM MERROW BEARE GREEN
OCKLEY SHERE

The end of the Second World War in 1945 brought at least prospects for some return to normal life. Two years later Ralph, now in his mid-seventies, re-started the Leith Hill Festival. The young assistant conductor wrote of his chief:

He has a wonderful gift for extracting the very best out of his singers and players. He has a great love and respect for the musical amateur and this feeling being reciprocated, he is able to draw more music from them than they themselves are aware they possess.

His whole demeanour shows what is wanted, and he seems to possess other hidden methods of communication that defy analysis. There is no doubt that his actual beat is sometimes difficult to see, but he seems to be able to keep his forces together by sheer gigantic will-power.

October 1947 brought Ralph's seventy-fifth birthday and the fiftieth anniversary of his and Adeline's marriage.

He had found a small gold locket for her in London, plain enough he hoped for her to care to wear.

At home with Foxy, one of the longest-lived, most intelligent and favourite of Ralph's succession of cats

94

Before the war's end, Ralph had begun his Sixth Symphony. By July 1946 the music was sufficiently complete to ask his old pupil Michael Mullinar to play it through at 'The White Gates'. Ursula wrote:

Ralph invited about twenty people to hear it. Michael played the symphony twice to the small audience. After they had left, we had supper, then Michael played again.

Sometime while we had been listening there had been rain, and by now the evening was brilliant with evening light and the colour of everything in the room was intensified. Adeline's crimson Indian shawl, her face, the music paper on the piano were luminous points in the dusk.

Michael played a song of his own, a setting of Waller's 'Old Age'. Ralph sang it through, reading over his shoulder:

'The soul's dark cottage, battered and decayed,
Lets in new light through chinks that time hath made
Stronger by weakness, wiser men become
As they draw near to their eternal home.
Leaving the old, both worlds at once they view
That stand upon the threshold of the new. . . .'

Then Michael played the Symphony again, the scherzo clear as ice and the last movement leading out into space. He had an uncanny power of being able to suggest Ralph's orchestration, and each of the many times he had played the work it had been with unflagging excitement and inspiration.

Because of that day Ralph dedicated the Symphony to him.

Ralph spent months revising the Symphony. In June 1947 Mullinar played it again. After still more revision, the first performance was conducted by Adrian Boult in April 1948.

He was starting to have trouble with his hearing— almost certainly a delayed result of exposure to the guns in France in 1918. By late 1947 Ursula noticed

Ralph's deafness was beginning to be a positive nuisance to him—particularly at the extremes of the musical range.

He was almost always too busy with people and things that were near to miss those who were not. Perhaps Gustav was the only exception, the one friend he never ceased to miss.

(*left*) Unveiling a tablet on Holst's Birthplace at Cheltenham, 1949.

(*right*) At the Gloucester Festival of 1950 with Jean Stewart (for whom he had written a String Quartet) and Ursula.

His interest in folk dancing remained as keen as ever

He was usually up by six in the morning, and so he had an hour and a half of quiet time for music before breakfast. After breakfast he took his letters to read to Adeline, and then he read 'The Times'. By nine he was back in his study, and there he stayed until lunch at half past twelve.

The afternoon was a quiet time—a little reading aloud, a sleep, gardening, or a walk—then tea and more work in the study . . . till supper time—a flexible feast adjusted to fit in with any broadcast to which they wanted to listen.

If there was no music or no play they cared for, Ralph would read, sleep, and perhaps go back to the study for another hour before bedtime.

For the English Folk Dance and Song Society's Committee there were meetings, library committees, and Editorial Boards to be attended; annual meetings of the English Hymnal Committee, concerts given by the Committee for the Promotion of New Music to hear, CEMA [forerunner of the Arts Council], British Council, and Surrey Education Committee meetings. Though he went only to those which he knew would produce some particular matter he should hear or speak about, it all took up a great deal of time. . . .

When he came to London he usually contrived to combine work and pleasure, going on from a meeting to a concert or a film. But for some concerts or operas he felt justified in making a special expedition. One of these was the first performance of Britten's opera Peter Grimes at Sadler's Wells . . .

He managed to do a great deal of reading. Both he and Adeline had . . . rediscovered and enjoyed Trollope's novels, they re-read Dickens, George Eliot, and Hardy as well as anything new they could get. Penguin books, library books, borrowed books all streamed into the house, and there was always one book being read aloud.

Ralph's opera *The Pilgrim's Progress*, forty years in the making, had been finished at last in 1949. His old friend Steuart Wilson, now Deputy General Director of Covent Garden, resolved to mount it there in 1951.

With Sir Steuart and Lady Wilson at a rehearsal in April 1951

The conductor was Leonard Hancock. Ursula wrote:

Ralph had insisted on a young conductor who would work right through the rehearsals, rather than a well known and busy star conductor who would come in at the end. Hancock knew his music thoroughly, and he understood from the first exactly what Ralph wanted.

The Pilgrim in prison

Ursula wrote:

. . . I understood how fearful this culmination of years of intense work translating vision into music and drama must be for the composer, who is at the mercy of many non-musical factors: for if the production, the designs, or the lighting do not please, it is more than probable that these will come before the music in critical appraisal.

Their worst fears were realized. One critic wrote:

It is hard to imagine a job worse done. The House Beautiful and the friendly landscapes amounted to no more than pale sentimental calendar art. Vanity Fair looked like a scene from the Dick Whittington pantomime. The delineation of lust and frivolity was enough to send one to the nearest convent in the hope of a gayer time. The lighting was uniformly atrocious. When Pilgrim was supposed to descry with effort a distant light, he was hit full in the face by a blinding spotlight.

Conductor and composer after the first performance. They know it had not succeeded.

Ralph's young friend Michael Kennedy was to write:

Its failure, and the misunderstanding of its nature, wounded the composer more deeply than anything else in his career.

In recent years everything had become more difficult for Adeline. Ursula wrote:

. . . Her eyes troubled her, and it was becoming an effort to have her chair wheeled out into the garden. . . .

She was visibly nourished by Ralph's presence; or perhaps she saved every scrap of strength for him. For when he was out of the room or away, she withdrew almost entirely, sitting bowed in her chair—silent, eyes closed, and drooping like a bird in a frozen winter night: reviving when he came in to talk and listen, though even then it often seemed an almost unendurable effort.

Her eightieth birthday, in July 1950, had passed without any possible celebration.

On 30 April 1951 the performance of 'Pilgrim' was broadcast. It went better on the stage that night, and Ralph came home happy to think that Adeline had been able to hear it.

She had tried to listen, but it was apparent that it had been too much for her: she was tired, and almost unable to speak. But by the next morning she was better again.

She seemed strong enough for him to leave her on 10 May, to attend a London University rehearsal of *Toward the Unknown Region*. There he was joined by Ursula, who wrote of the aftermath:

I saw him off at Waterloo. Soon after I got home, he telephoned to say that Adeline had died in the afternoon. She had died with her women round her, like a queen in a story. She had died while the fresh voices of the students sang: 'All waits undreamed of in that region, that inaccessible land.'

When I went to her room next day, taking flowers from the garden, she looked as fragile as the body of a small bird. Her early beauty, her lively mind, her austere discipline, her tenderness and edged wit had dissolved and left no trace on the wrecked face that lay between hyacinths and jonquils on the pillow.

After the funeral . . . Ralph came home to a frenzy of activity. He wanted everything done at once. He tore up letters and photographs, cleared desks, distributed jewellery to Adeline's nieces, answered letters, and attacked every problem with concentration and speed.

After he had worked through all the early summer, Ursula got him away for a holiday to Kent and Romney Marsh. She arranged that, during their absence, 'The White Gates' should be thoroughly redecorated from top to bottom—a task impossible during Adeline's last years.

In 1947 the conductor Ernest Irving had written to ask Ralph to write music for the film about Scott's expedition to the South Pole. Ralph was at first reluctant to commit so much time. But Irving was persuasive, and the idea of the strange world of ice and storm began to fascinate him. . . .

Pictures of the Scott expedition lay about the house, and work was begun. Ralph became more and more upset as he read about the inefficiencies of the organization: he despised heroism that risked lives unnecessarily . . . Apart from this, he was excited by the demands which the setting of the film made on his invention—to find musical equivalents for the physical sensations of ice, of wind blowing over the great uninhabited desolation, of stubborn and impassable ridges of black and ice-covered rock, and to suggest man's endeavour to overcome the rigours of this bleak land and to match mortal spirit against elements. . . . Ralph won his point with the Studio about the use of voices to suggest desolation and icy winds . . . He had already begun to think that he might use the music for an Antarctic Symphony.

A still from 'Scott of the Antarctic'.

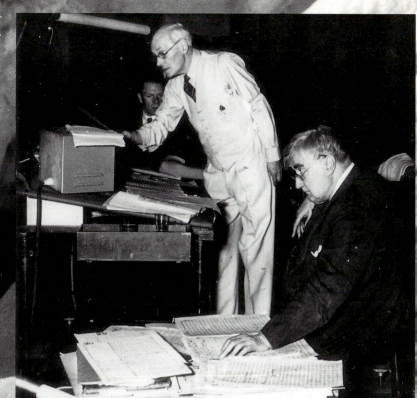

Ernest Irving conducting Ralph's music for 'Scott of the Antarctic' at Ealing Studios, 1948.

After the film was finished and shown, he had begun to recast and extend its music to make 'Sinfonia Antartica'—his Seventh Symphony. It was dedicated to Ernest Irving, and finished in 1952.

It was the autumn of Ralph's eightieth birthday. His old Cambridge friend G. M. Trevelyan (a distinguished historian and another OM) wrote to him:

All England is rejoicing over your birthday, and you may be sure I do too. We have both achieved very much what we were respectively dreaming of at Seatoller in 1895. We have had fortunate lives in a very unfortunate age.

With Ralph listening in the Free Trade Hall, Manchester, John Barbirolli rehearsed the Hallé Orchestra for the first performance of 'Sinfonia Antartica' on 14 January 1953.

For some time Ralph had wanted to marry Ursula. One night in January 1953, after a Barbirolli performance of *Tristan und Isolde* at Covent Garden, she accepted him. They did not announce the engagement in the press, but sent a card to close friends.

URSULA WOOD,
57, GORDON MANSIONS,
TORRINGTON PLACE, W C.1.

RALPH VAUGHAN WILLIAMS,
THE WHITE GATES,
DORKING, SURREY.

YOU WILL, WE THINK, NOT BE SURPRISED TO HEAR THAT WE HAVE DECIDED TO MARRY SHORTLY.

OUR ADDRESSES WILL BE AS ABOVE FOR THE PRESENT, TILL WE FIND A SUITABLE HOUSE.

PLEASE GIVE US YOUR BLESSING.

The wedding took place on 7 February 1953 at St. Pancras Vestry Chapel.

Although Ralph had said he was too old to travel ever again, he had acquired a new passport in the summer of 1951.

In 1952 with Ursula he had revisited Mont St. Michel and Chartres—unseen since his first trip abroad with his mother seventy years earlier.

In the spring of 1953, he and Ursula went for a delayed wedding trip to Italy.

Two years later they went to Greece. On Mikonos Ralph bought a conch shell and taught himself to blow this oldest and newest musical instrument.

They would live in London:

We had done some house-hunting, and looked at all sorts of possible and impossible places.

10 Hanover Terrace [above, the two left-hand bays under the portico], Regent's Park, was empty. It had been rebuilt inside, and now had central heating installed. It overlooked the lake and the Park, and it had a garden.

It was exactly what we wanted—quiet, central, and beautiful—so we took the Crown Lease for twenty-one years. It gladdened my heart when Ralph said it seemed rather short, and asked if it could be extended when it expired. We felt immortal.

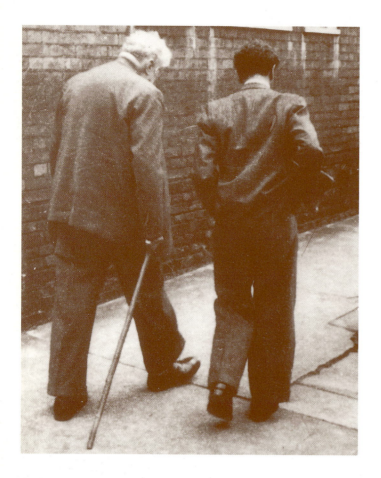

One of Ralph's closest friends of a younger generation was Gerald Finzi. The Gloucester Festival in September 1953 included works by both. It gave a chance for conversations throughout the week.

Roy Douglas had been helping him for some years. Roy had developed an unerring understanding of Ralph's calligraphy, which he translated into his own clear writing—as well as coming to play unfinished works through, advising on questionable points of instrumentation, and bringing all his skill and musicianship to Ralph's help.

Just before preliminary rehearsals for the 1953 Gloucester Festival at the Royal College of Music, Ralph had written to the critic Frank Howes:

If you happen to be passing the R.C.M. on Thursday at 2.45 you will find Roy Douglas, playing through a new tune by me, and David Willcocks, to see if he would like to do it at Worcester next year.

In December 1953 the London Philharmonic Orchestra under Sir Adrian Boult completed the first recording of all Vaughan Williams Symphonies then written. Ralph and Ursula were at Kingsway Hall throughout the sessions. Ralph gave the performers generous praise, and some of his spoken words were included on one of the discs. Ursula wrote of the sessions:

It was both tedious and exhilarating: tedious in the gaps and waits, the murky greenish blue tipped-up seats, the rumble of trains passing under the hall and disorganizing the music, the cold weather and the sandwich meals; exhilarating in the concentration, the repetition of each passage—first live, then recorded, then live again—with hearing sharpened to take in every variation of clarity, balance, and tempo.

Ralph at Hanover Terrace with special gramophone equipment designed to help his hearing.

Ralph's 'new tune' for the 1954 Worcester Festival was the Christmas cantata *This Day*—or (as he liked to call it) *Hodie*. For the libretto he had turned to Ursula, who recalled:

In 1952 he had told me that he thought there should be another Christmas work, and that it would be fun to write one.

I said that I had compiled a programme of Christmas poems, using linking passages from the gospels, and I had put it away and forgotten about it.

When I took it to Dorking, Ralph got out his own scenario, and the two were almost identical. From this we built up the libretto for 'Hodie'.

Despite worsening hearing, Ralph was persuaded to conduct the first performance of *Hodie*.

At rehearsals he relied on the Cathedral organist, David Willcocks, to help ascertain complex balances down the long nave and aisles of Worcester Cathedral.

Hodie was dedicated to Herbert Howells (who came to Worcester to conduct his *Missa Sabrinensis*). He wrote to Ralph:

Nothing has ever touched me more than this dedication.

A new excitement came
on our horizon when Ralph
woke one morning saying, 'We've
never seen the Grand Canyon—what
shall we do about it?'

By the afternoon we had the Canyon in
sight: for Keith Falkner, then a professor of
music at Cornell University, came to lunch. Ralph
spoke of Colorado, and Keith suggested an American
lecture tour . . .

Before long Ralph (through Keith's good offices) was
invited to be visiting professor at Cornell for the autumn
term of 1954—to include rehearsing and conducting his works—
and a lecture tour through the United States was designed to let
us see the Pacific and the Grand Canyon.

Ralph's Eighth Symphony (begun in 1954) was his briefest. But it spoke profoundly of renewed vigour.

Sir John Barbirolli (to whom the Eighth was dedicated) spent the early months of 1956 rehearsing it for the première on 2 May.

Ralph and Ursula went to Manchester for the rehearsals. They were joined by the young critic Michael Kennedy, who was to write the definitive study of Ralph's music.

Ursula wrote:

At a very late stage in the composition of it, I had been innocently guilty of causing an expensive addition to be made to the already large percussion group.

Seeing that there was a performance of Turandot *(an opera I had never heard) I suggested that we should go. The only tickets left were for the front row of the stalls, and there we sat.*

Ralph was fascinated by the sound of the tuned gongs, so the moment the lights went up he lifted the curtain that hides the orchestra from the audience, and beckoned to the player. They spent the whole interval in conference.

Next morning the gongs were added to the score, where a note says —

'Gongs are not absolutely essential, but their inclusion is highly desirable.'

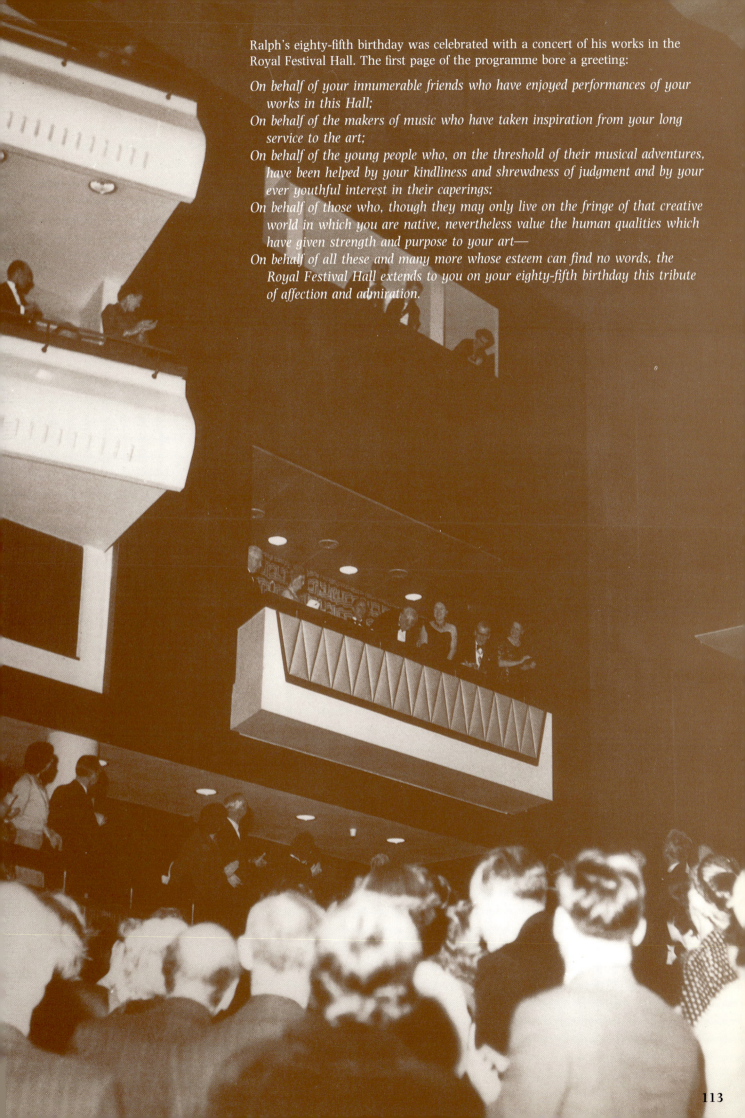

Ralph's eighty-fifth birthday was celebrated with a concert of his works in the Royal Festival Hall. The first page of the programme bore a greeting:

On behalf of your innumerable friends who have enjoyed performances of your works in this Hall;

On behalf of the makers of music who have taken inspiration from your long service to the art;

On behalf of the young people who, on the threshold of their musical adventures, have been helped by your kindliness and shrewdness of judgment and by your ever youthful interest in their caperings;

On behalf of those who, though they may only live on the fringe of that creative world in which you are native, nevertheless value the human qualities which have given strength and purpose to your art—

On behalf of all these and many more whose esteem can find no words, the Royal Festival Hall extends to you on your eighty-fifth birthday this tribute of affection and admiration.

Ralph's Ninth Symphony had found its beginning in impressions of Salisbury Plain.

(from *Pictorial Architecture of the British Isles*, given to Ralph by his mother for Christmas, 1883, and in his library ever afterwards)

Another element in the Ninth Symphony had come in the summer of 1957, with the hearing of a Flügelhorn on holiday in Austria.

In March 1958 the newest Symphony was rehearsed by the Royal Philharmonic Orchestra for its première. After a photo-call with the conductor Sir Malcolm Sargent and the Flügelhorn player David Mason, Ralph noted:

The Flügel man showed me at rehearsal that unless I allowed a minimum of vibrato, the tone would sound hard, rather like a bad horn.

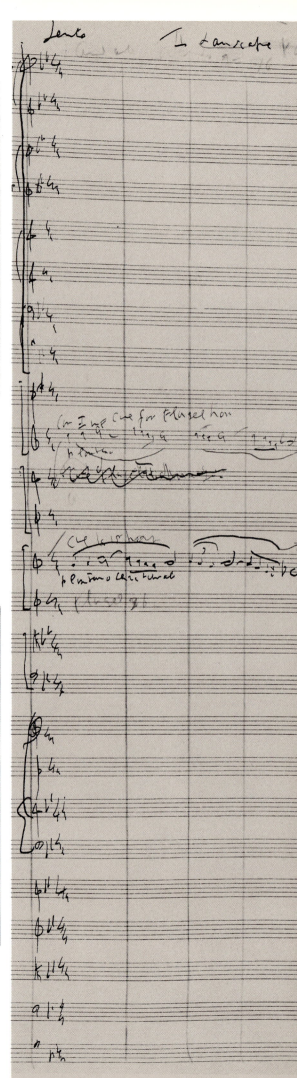

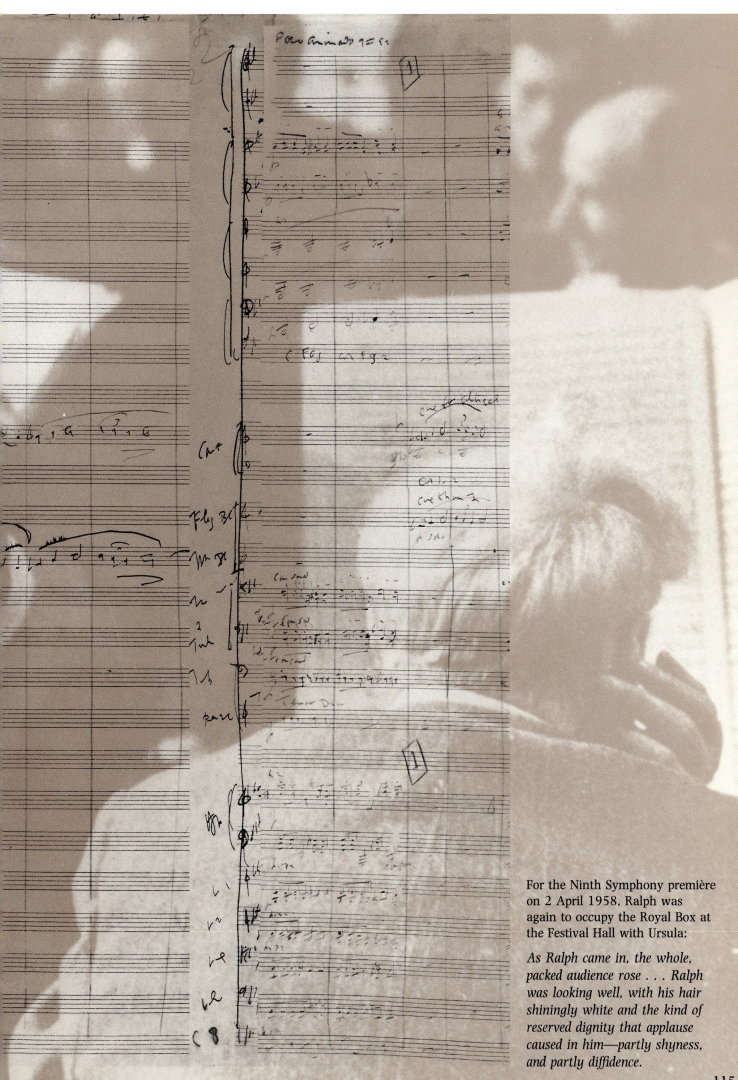

For the Ninth Symphony première on 2 April 1958, Ralph was again to occupy the Royal Box at the Festival Hall with Ursula:

As Ralph came in, the whole, packed audience rose . . . Ralph was looking well, with his hair shiningly white and the kind of reserved dignity that applause caused in him—partly shyness, and partly diffidence.

Several projects were incomplete.
One was a Cello Concerto.

*Ralph died on 26 August 1958. His ashes were buried
in Westminster Abbey on 17 September 1958.*

Eheu Fugaces
Horace, Odes II. xiv. 1

Swiftly they pass, the flying years,
no prayer can stay their course,
here is the road each man must tread
be he of royal blood or lowly birth.
Vainly we shun the battle's roar
the perilous sea, the fever-laden breezes,
soon shall we reach our journey's end
and trembling cross the narrow stream of death.
Land, house, and wife must all be left,
the cherished trees be all cut down,
strangers shall lord it in our home
and squander all our store.

Translated by Ralph for the Abinger Pageant 1938

The end of the tale, as shown in
this book's distinguished predecessor
by Ursula Vaughan Williams and John Lunn.

Sources and Acknowledgements

THE first and greatest of this book's benefactors is the composer's widow, Ursula Vaughan Williams. Her help over information, wording, and photographs has been such that I asked her to share the authorship: this she characteristically refused. But she has, at my particular request, expressed her thoughts directly in the Preface.

Mrs Vaughan Williams also secured the generous help of her collaborator in this book's predecessor, Dr John Lunn. Dr Lunn placed all his materials and knowledge at my disposal, and I have gained richly from them.

Failing a new text from Ursula Vaughan Williams, I could not do better than turn to the pages of her unique memoir *R. V. W.* (Oxford University Press, 1964). Unless otherwise noted, quotations herein are taken from that source. All quotations of more than a few words are printed in italics.

Quotations from other sources and photographs are listed by page (generally from top to bottom and left to right) with all information available. Copyright holders are cited in parentheses, and grateful thanks given them all for permission to reproduce the images. The demanding work of copying old photographs was in the skilled hands of Michael Dudley at the Ashmolean Museum, Oxford.

2   *Erasmus Darwin* by Joseph Wright of Derby (National Portrait Gallery, London)
    View in the Grounds of Ashbourne Hall by John Glover, engraved by William Byrne, *detail*: frontispiece to Erasmus Darwin's *A Plan for the Conduct of Female Education in Boarding Schools*, 1797

3   *Josiah Wedgwood* by Sir Joshua Reynolds, 1782 (Wedgwood Museum, Barlaston, Stoke-on-Trent)
    The Pottery at Etruria in Josiah Wedgwood's Time, anonymous drawing (Wedgwood Museum)

4   *The Wedgwood Sisters*, anonymous drawing *c.*1850
    Margaret Wedgwood, anonymous photograph dated 27 May 1856
    Leith Hill Place

5   *The Hall at Tanhurst*, anonymous drawing *c.*1845
    Arthur Vaughan Williams, photo by Maria Budge, Wells, *c.*1855

6   *Down Ampney Church, c.*1870
    Arthur Vaughan Williams

7   *Margaret Vaughan Williams with Hervey*, Aug. 1869

8   *Down Ampney Register of Baptisms*, 1872
    Down Ampney Vicarage, photo by National Monuments Record, 30 Sept. 1969 (Crown copyright)
    Ralph, photo by W. Usherwood, Dorking, Sept. 1876

9   *Arthur Vaughan Williams, c.*1874

10 *Leith Hill Place*
    Margaret Vaughan Williams, later photo from a group

11 *Leith Hill Place Servants*, photo by W. Plammer, Dorking, June 1895
    Hervey and Meggie, photo by W. Usherwood, Dorking, Sept. 1876
    Ralph, photo by W. Usherwood, Dorking, Sept. 1876

12 *Ralph*, photo by Day & Son, Bournemouth
    The Robin's Nest (British Library Add MS 54186, fo. 2)
    Charles Darwin

13 *Leith Hill Place*

14 *Ralph*, photo by Jas. Russell & Sons, Worthing
    Pages from the Darwin family *Shakespeare*, inherited by Ralph
    Overture 'The Galoshes of Happienes'

15 *Snow woods in mooonlight*, post card photo by Charnaux Frères, Geneva
    Mark Cook in the Kitchen Garden at Leith Hill Place, photo by Adeline Vaughan Williams, *c.*1897

16 *Mont St. Michel*, photo by Martin Hürlimann, *c.*1920
    Hervey, photo by W. & A. H. Fry, Brighton, 1885
    Ralph, photo by W. & A. H. Fry, Brighton, Mar. 1885

17 *Meggie*, photo by Day & Son, Bournemouth
    Pictorial Architecture of the British Isles by Rev H. H. Bishop, SPCK, n.d., detail from p. 50

18 *Field House School, St Aubyns*, photo by National Monuments Record, 25 Aug. 1969 (Crown copyright)
    Edge of the Sussex Downs, post card photo by Judge's, Hastings

19 *Field House staff and boys*, photo by W. & A. H. Fry, Brighton, 1886
    Ralph, photo by Van der Velde, Regent Street, London, 1885

20 *Charterhouse*, 1888
    Robinites, 1889

21 *Concert at Charterhouse, c.*1888

22 *Ralph*, photo by G. West, Godalming, Apr. 1890
    Leith Hill Place
    Royal College of Music, old building, photo by Cassell & Co.

23 *Sir Hubert Parry*, photo by Histed, 1898
    Gustav Mahler, silhouette by Hans Schliessmann

24 *Bicycling* with one of Adeline Fisher's brothers
    Trinity College, Cambridge
    Adeline at The Vicarage, Hooton Roberts, Yorks.

25 *Seatoller Log Book* drawing by Maurice Amos, 1895
    Ralph and 'Randolph' Wedgwood, 1896

26 *Charles Villiers Stanford*, photo by Herbert Lambert
    Gustav Holst

27 *Ralph*
    2, St Barnabas Villas, South Lambeth

28 *Adeline Fisher, c.*1896

29 *Croquet at The Vicarage, Hooton Roberts: Nicholas and Margaret Gatty, with Ralph*
    Chamber music at Hooton Roberts
    Adeline at the water's edge

30 *Adeline and Ralph*
    Ralph at Bolzano, photo by Adeline, Dec. 1897

31 *10, Barton Street, Westminster*
    Quotation, bottom right, from *The Works of Ralph Vaughan Williams*, by Michael Kennedy, 2nd edn., OUP, 1980, p. 44

32 *Adeline*, photo by G. C. Beresford, London, 1908
    Ralph on Stony Ground

33 *The Prioress's Tale*, by Sir Edward Burne-Jones, detail (Delaware Art Museum, Samuel and Mary R. Bancroft Memorial, 1935)

34 *Mark Cook and his Granddaughter*, photo by Adeline, 1897
    Linden Lea, from the Sketchbook

35 *Ralph*, photo by Scott & Wilkinson, Cambridge